Collective Equity

We are deeply humbled and grateful as we thank our Lord and Savior, Jesus Christ. He has blessed us with many opportunities to pursue and accomplish our dreams despite challenges and our own crisis of confidence that we have faced during this process of writing Collective Equity. *We thank Him for His grace, love, and mercy toward us. We thank each other for the mutuality and reciprocity that we continue to give so that both of us are fortified in all that we do. Our friendship has grown out of us learning from and with each other as champions for equity. We will always be the collective for each other in love and in respect.*

From Nicole:

Collective Equity *could not have occurred without the love, patience, and understanding of my family, Stan Law, and my pride and joy, Kyle Jordan Law. I appreciate the times when I needed a quiet space and to get away to write with Sonja Alexander. I thank the two of you for enduring the endless energy it took for us to finally complete the writing process. I could not have done this task without the encouragement and continuous prayers from my tribe; and you know who you are. And I thank my pastor and guide, Pastor Kim Outlaw, who was a shepherd who earnestly and faithfully empowered us to press on despite hardships through her words and the word of God. To my queen, now my angel, Bernice B. Smith, who taught me to have relentless faith to be strong in the Lord, in the power of his might, and taught me that there is nothing too hard for him: I would not be the woman I am without your direction and your belief in me. May you rest in peace.*

From Sonja:

The process of writing Collective Equity *has been daunting, rewarding, and truly a gift to my soul and spirit. I dedicate this book to so many who encouraged me along the way but only have the space to thank a few. First and foremost, my parents John and Mildred Hollins, who are resting in heaven. Their love continuously stays with me and they are ever-present in everything I do, all that I am, my hopes and dreams, and who they desired me to be. To my deep inspiration who continues to push me forward no matter how tired I may be, Autumn Eliza Alexander, my amazing daughter: You are my everything and I will continue to run the race because of my love and dedication to you. To my wonderful siblings (Teresa, Jerome, John, Tekki, Mary, Victor, Earl, and Tammie) who have always been my champions. Every night during the process of writing we prayed, and you were committed to holding the both of us up when we were weary but very hopeful. And to my loving Michael, who continues to sacrifice, be patient, and believe in me when I often do not know how to believe in myself. You always remind me of my why. As well, to my amazing friend group who hold me down and keep me laughing and grounded through life's ups and downs: I give my love to all of you.*

Collective Equity

A Movement for Creating Communities Where We All Can Breathe

Sonja Hollins-Alexander
Nicole Law

Foreword by John Almarode

FOR INFORMATION:

Corwin

A SAGE Company

2455 Teller Road

Thousand Oaks, California 91320

(800) 233-9936

www.corwin.com

SAGE Publications Ltd.

1 Oliver's Yard

55 City Road

London, EC1Y 1SP

United Kingdom

SAGE Publications India Pvt. Ltd.

B 1/I 1 Mohan Cooperative Industrial Area

Mathura Road, New Delhi 110 044

India

SAGE Publications Asia-Pacific Pte. Ltd.

18 Cross Street #10-10/11/12

China Square Central

Singapore 048423

President: Mike Soules

Associate Vice President and
Editorial Director: Monica Eckman

Program Director and Publisher: Dan Alpert

Senior Content Development Editor: Lucas Schleicher

Associate Content Development Editor: Mia Rodriguez

Production Editor: Megha Negi

Copy Editor: Diana Breti

Typesetter: Hurix digital

Cover Designer: Gail Buschman

Marketing Manager: Sharon Pendergast

Editorial Intern: Ricardo Ramirez

ISBN: 978-1-0718-4474-8

This book is printed on acid-free paper.

22 23 24 25 10 9 8 7 6 5 4 3 2

Contents

Visit the companion website at
resources.corwin.com/CollectiveEquity
for downloadable resources.

Foreword

A critical discussion or dialogue requires several conditions to be met for each individual to successfully participate:

1. Openness to engage in the exchange of ideas and information

2. Prior knowledge related to the specific topic

3. A shared language around the topic

4. A space in which to carry out the discussion or dialogue

5. Respect of the other participants and their viewpoints and perspectives

These conditions are interrelated and together provide an opportunity to see and experience different perspectives on a common topic. They are the variables that, together, create the potential to leave any critical discussion or dialogue enlightened, informed, and/or validated.

Conversations about equity in our schools and classrooms should not be an exception. However, entering into a critical discussion or dialogue around the equity of access and opportunity is risky at this particular time. This is highlighted by the increased number of bumper stickers, signs, newspaper articles, television broadcasts, local policies, and state and federal legislation focused on either promoting or protesting anything related to equity. School board meetings look less like civilized community engagement and more like cage matches held in government office buildings, all because fellow citizens want to ensure that young learners, the next generation of citizens, are not held accountable or punished for circumstances beyond their control.

Why is that? What is so threatening, provocative, egregious, or outrageous about the desire for every student to have equity of access and the opportunity to be the best version of themselves? What is so objectionable about ensuring that an 8-year-old has access to the highest level of learning possible? I really do not know. Call me naïve, but I have always operated on the assumption that the very thing we can all agree on is the value of fellow human beings, especially children, engaged in the collective pursuit of life, liberty, and happiness.

If critical discussions and dialogue generate the variables necessary for change, until we as a collective of human beings can engage in these conversations, the desire for every human being to have equity of access and opportunity to be the best version of themselves will remain a potential—never converted into the kinetic energy of change. Again, why is equity the exception? Certainly, if we can debate Ford versus Chevy, Nike versus Adidas, steak versus chicken, the Red Sox versus the Yankees, the value of a child should be easy to discuss. What is going on here?

Sonja Hollins-Alexander and Nicole Law, through their incredibly powerful work, have added to the critical discussion and dialogue on equity in our schools and classrooms. The subsequent pages of this book offer us the greatest possibility of moving the needle forward in our quest for an equitable tomorrow. Sonja and Nicole lay out a clear, concise, and actionable framework for building our individual *resilience to interrupt the barriers and beasts that perpetuate inequity in our schools and classrooms*, but transform the focus from us as individuals to our *collective strength and courage*. We are in this together. Furthermore, these two authors take and model an authentically humble approach, recognizing that we are all learners seeking to amplify our *knowledge, attitudes, and skills to building a thriving community that fulfills the promise of equity for all of us*. Equity is collective.

This framework in which you are about to be immersed provides the essential support or, as they identify them, the "equity pathways and equity pavers":

1. Come together with a high level of openness to celebrate our differences

2. Equip us with knowledge about equity so that we do not rely on stereotypes, myths, misconceptions, misunderstandings, and rumors

3. Develop a shared language for engaging in the hard work of collective equity

4. Create a safe space for the hard work of equity

5. Ensure that the framework does not lose sight of the launching point for collective equity: a genuine respect for fellow human beings

The critical discussions and dialogue about equity are difficult for many individuals. Some folks find it difficult because they are, to be quite honest, racist. Some folks find it difficult because they lack awareness of their own privilege and, therefore, are resistant to the conversation. These individuals are unconsciously unskilled. Others, like myself, do not believe they are racist and do not lack self-awareness about privilege, but feel unequipped with the knowledge, attitudes, and skills to engage in the quest for collective equity without creating more harm than good. These individuals are consciously unskilled. These three categories above represent the ideal audience for this book. Although two of the three will be difficult to engage, the challenge is worth it. It is time! And, if you are reading this Foreword, you have taken the first step. Keep reading!

I want to close out this Foreword with some very personal sharing. I am a white, heterosexual, middle-class male who is also a tenured professor at a major state university. I now find myself writing the Foreword for a book on collective equity. Yeah, this moment is not lost on me. Some would argue that the very last thing we need is someone with my characteristics jumping into this conversation. But let me share some very personal information with you that frames my perspective on collective equity—my own personal equity pathways, equity pavers, and elements of the Collective Equity Framework.

As a teenager, I was horribly bullied. So much so that I feared for my safety at school. Although my teachers did offer me a refuge, I also developed a friendship with a senior basketball player who not only was my friend, but protected me. She took me under her wing, mentored me, and supported me. I cannot recall specifically how we became such good friends or explain why our particular friendship evolved the way that it did. What I can tell you is that she was and still is someone very important to me. And, up until recently, I never felt compelled to point out that she was Black. Her friendship literally changed my life. That is all I saw and all I knew. But today, with the national narrative so divided around our individual characteristics (e.g., gender, race, ethnicity, sexual orientation, socioeconomic status), I am consciously unskilled to step up to the occasion and engage in the quest for collective equity. Not just for me, but for the people that I love, care about, and who have made an immeasurable impact on my life; not because of the color of their skin or their country of origin, but because they are human beings; not because I feel the need to apologize for being white, but because that young child in the fifth seat of the third row deserves equity of access and opportunity to the highest learning possible because it is the right thing to do! I believe this is one of the reasons I was asked to write this Foreword. I know I am coming from a place of privilege. But, I want to develop the knowledge, attitudes, and skills to leverage that privilege to ensure my community, my school, and my classroom are thriving learning communities that fulfill the promise of equity for all learners.

I am betting on the fact that I am not alone in this quest.

John Almarode

Acknowledgments

We have often referred to writing this book as preparing for the birth of something absolutely earth-shattering. This birth of collective equity has come with myriad people supporting us behind the scenes. This birthing is now our reality because of the support, encouragement, and sacrifice we have been afforded by those we acknowledge below.

To our editor, Dan Alpert, our warm demander: We want to acknowledge and thank you for every conversation, editing suggestion, and partnership on this journey. We will never be the same because of you. You unearthed the best parts of who we are, and we are forever grateful. A shout out to Mia Rodriguez, who has been a coach and cheerleader and provided us with best practices in how to represent collective equity. You have been responsive to our needs and patient as we learned along the way. Lucas Schleicher, your immediacy brought vision and representation to our thoughts and ideas and we are thankful that you are on our team. We want to thank our cover designer, Gail Buschman, for her creativity and commitment to breathing life to the title based on her visual inspiration.

We want to thank our Corwin family for their continued support and encouragement. Lydia Chavira, your continuous dedication and sacrifice to make *Collective Equity* come to fruition is a heartfelt gift that will never go unnoticed. We want to thank Monique Corridori and Katie Hann for ensuring educators across America would experience our passion for equity and our deep-seated commitment to mitigating educational oppression. To our partners on the sales, learning, marketing, and editorial teams: We thank you for elevating us, positioning the work, identifying ways to support us through this process, and being available and ever-present. To Michael Soules: We express gratitude for your transparency and vulnerability as you question, inquire, and pave the way for equity to be the center of who we are as an organization at

Corwin/SAGE. Your fierce leadership means a lot to us as employees and is even more meaningful to us as Black women.

We want to acknowledge the deep equity team for the equity partnerships and riveting conversations that contributed to our growth and increased our equity stamina. Thank you for being real, raw, and bringing relevance to this work. Doug Fisher and Nancy Frey, you continue to serve as models as we have observed your unrelenting commitment to bring knowledge, support, and value to educators across the world. It brings us joy as we recognize equity as the through-line in all your bodies of work; it is part of our evolution to strengthen our voices as we strive toward the promise of equity in our schools. We stand on the shoulders of an equity giant, Gary Howard, whose gentleness, strength, wisdom, and equity capacity have enabled us to continue this beautiful yet arduous work that has exposed our shared truths: passion yet equity fatigue because we have not seen and/or experienced the promise of equity. We love you for your generativity to this work.

To John Almarode, our thought partner, researcher, inspiration, and friend: We thank you for the ways in which you were present and showed up for us. You were always there when we needed you the most through our uncertainties and spaces of learning.

We gratefully acknowledge the contributions of the equity voices represented in *Collective Equity*:

- Dr. Theresa Yeldell, Principal, Banner Prep High School, Milwaukee, Wisconsin

- Dr. Denita Harris, Chief Diversity, Equity and Inclusion Officer, Indianapolis, Indiana

- Ms. Joi Kilpatrick, Principal, William M. Boyd Elementary School, Atlanta, Georgia

- Mr. Isaiah Johnson, Director of Equity, Family Engagement, and Outreach, Auburn, Washington

- Mr. Stan Law, Principal, George Washington High School, Indianapolis, Indiana

Publisher's Acknowledgments

Corwin gratefully acknowledges the contributions of the following reviewers:

John Almarode
Associate Professor, Executive Director of Teaching and Learning, and
    Author of *How Learning Works*
James Madison University
Harrisonburg, VA

Waldo V. Alvarado
Director of Equity and Diversity
Reading School District
Reading, PA

Douglas Fisher
Professor of Educational Leadership, Teacher Leader, and Author
    of *The Distance Learning Playbook*
Health Sciences High and Middle College
San Diego, CA

Gary Howard
Activist, Consultant, and Author of *We Can't Lead Where We
    Won't Go*
Seattle, WA

James McKay
School Superintendent
Community High School District 117
Lake Vila, IL

Felipe Sepulveda
Professor
Universidad Catolica de la Santísma Concepción
Concepción, Chile

Ron Wahlen
Director of Digital Teaching and Learning
Durham Public Schools
Durham, NC

Theresa W. Yeldell
High School Principal
Milwaukee Public Schools
Milwaukee, WI

About the Authors

Dr. Sonja Hollins-Alexander is the senior director of professional learning for Corwin. She has been in the field of education for 28 years, with 22 of those being in educational leadership roles in schools, districts, universities, and professional learning organizations. During her professional career, she has provided service in the following K–12 positions: school social worker, teacher, teacher on special assignment, assistant principal, principal, coordinator, assistant director and director of professional learning, and chief of staff in Metro Atlanta, Georgia, school districts. Dr. Hollins-Alexander continues to serve in an advocacy capacity through her membership on numerous nonprofit boards including Camp Fire Boys and Girls, affiliated with United Way nonprofit organizations; Learning Forward Georgia and Learning Forward National; and, most recently, she was selected to serve as an inaugural board member for Leflore Legacy Academy charter school in the Mississippi Delta (Greenwood, MS).

Through her professional journey, Dr. Hollins-Alexander has presented on numerous educational topics, such as visible learning, online professional development, professional learning communities, data analysis and use, common formative assessments, equitable learning structures, and culturally fortifying practices. She has demonstrated her knowledge and skills for educational excellence by developing district-based coaches and implementing a personalized learning coaching framework, serving as a lead coach for a district-based coaching endorsement program, and acting as a dissertation chair and committee member at the university level. In addition, she has a keen ability to engage in focused strategies that create effective and impactful organizational structures, such as strategic planning, organizational analysis, policy development, curriculum development and implementation, facilitation of adult learning, leadership/executive coaching, and conference facilitation and design. She is fully engaged in the development and use of online collaborative/instructional platforms and instructional design of professional learning services. She is the author of *Online Professional Development Through Virtual Learning Communities* (Corwin, 2013). Dr. Hollins-Alexander has a doctorate in curriculum and instruction and has received numerous awards for her educational pursuits, including State of GA School Greatest Gains in Student Achievement Award, Recognized American School Counseling Association Model Program Award, National Staff Development Council Shirley Hord Award, and Georgia Distinguished Principal Award.

As the senior director of professional learning for Corwin (a global professional learning organization), Sonja is committed to the design and implementation of evidence-based professional learning services that positively impact teaching and learning. She resides in Atlanta, Georgia, and her favorite activity is spending time with her family and her beautiful and brilliant daughter, Autumn Eliza Alexander.

Sonja can be reached at Sonja.HollinsAlexander@Corwin.com.

Dr. Nicole Law is a passionate educator who provides professional learning to schools and districts across the country. As a Corwin professional learning consultant, Nicole presents content on culturally fortifying practices, dimensions of equity and creating equitable teaching spaces, teacher clarity, visible learning, professional learning communities, literacy instruction, leadership improvement practices and structures, data analysis models, school improvement practices, metacognitive teaching and learning, strategies for success in cognitively rigorous instruction, and effective teaching methods for English learners.

Nicole has served as a curriculum coordinator for English language learners, cultural responsivity, AVID (Advancement via Individual Determination), district equity, and mathematics and science instruction in the Metropolitan School District of Wayne Township in Indianapolis, Indiana. In this position, Dr. Law created multi-layered professional development for teachers and administrators covering all aspects of directed programs and curricular areas. She has written curriculum in the areas of science, mathematics, and English language development. Nicole trained and supported administrators, teacher leaders, site coordinators, and school improvement teams in decision making for results, the data teams process, subgroup data dives, and gap reduction practices.

Dr. Law completed her doctorate in educational leadership and policy. She has received various recognitions throughout her career, including the 2008 National Milken Award from the state of Indiana. Nicole resides in Indianapolis, Indiana, with her husband and family and is a proud mother of her son, Kyle Law.

Nicole can be reached at Nicole.Law@Corwin.com.

Introduction

Can we breathe, can we talk, can we protest, can we have simultaneous truths, can we display anger, and can we admit to the crippling effects of inequity? The three words "I can't breathe" have echoed in the hearts, minds, and ears of Black Americans who fear being the next hashtag. This continues to fuel an outpouring of protests, an overwhelming cry for action, and urgent calls for social change. The asphyxiation of Black America has led to civic unrest. The unjust killings of Javier Ambler, Manuel Ellis, Elijah McClain, Eric Garner, and George Floyd as well as 70 other victims (Baker, Valentino-DeVries, Fernandez, & LaForgia, 2020) amount to a miscarriage of justice and a smothering of the human spirit.

If we can solve the inequities and the injustices in our society, then the knee that is on our necks will be lifted so we can show up in the fullness of who we are as a contributor to the beauty of the human race—the human race that collectively represents diversity, the ability to create social networks, and the capacity to love and care for others.

Schools are a microcosm of society, reflecting historical inequities and systemic structures of oppression. We must interrogate existing structures as well as systems, policies, and practices that suffocate the cultural excellence of all individuals. This is the premise of a free and public education.

There are 50.8 million students in American public schools; of these 50.8 million, white students represent 47 percent, Hispanic students represent 27 percent, Black students represent 15 percent, Asian students represent 5 percent, American Indian/Alaska Native students represent 1 percent, Pacific Islander students represent 0.4 percent, and students of two or more races represent 4 percent (Education Week Research Center, 2019).

Although the disparities that exist among Black, indigenous, and people of color (BIPOC) have endured for generations, they have been revealed with painful clarity in our schools today. Do our schools display the readiness to disrupt the barriers that have a significant impact on teaching and learning? We believe in the capacity of educators to address these staggering problems, but we must first come to terms with the sobering reality of disparity in our schools. Such disparities surface in the disproportionate representation of Black students in high-poverty schools, lack of access to college-ready courses such as Algebra II for BIPOC students, and lack of BIPOC representation in advanced placement (AP) courses (National School Boards Association, 2020; de Brey et al., 2019). The following data delineate disparities in American schools.

AMERICAN PUBLIC SCHOOLS EDUCATIONAL DISPARITIES (de Brey et al., 2019)	
Math and science disparities by race	One-quarter of high schools with the highest percentage of Black and Latino students do not offer Algebra II; a third of these schools do not offer Chemistry.
	Fewer than half of American Indian and Native Alaskan high school students have access to the full range of math and science courses in their high school.
Gifted and talented disparities by race	There is a growing opportunity gap in gifted and talented education; Black and Latino students represent only 26 percent of the students enrolled in gifted and talented education programs.
Advanced placement course disparities by race, language, and ability	Twenty-seven percent of Black and Latino students in our nation's high schools are enrolled in at least one AP course.
	English learners represent 5 percent of high school students. A mere 2 percent of these students are enrolled in at least one AP course.
	Students with disabilities served by IDEA represent 12 percent of high school students, whereas 2 percent of these students are enrolled in an AP course.
High school completion by immigration and socioeconomic status	On average, immigrant students and those from socioeconomically disadvantaged families receive fewer degrees, and a greater number display academic skills below grade level than do their more privileged peers (Gamoran, 2001).

Every state has a public school system and is accountable for providing a free education to every child. However, free for all does not mean subpar for some! Schools seek to promote diversity and disrupt discriminatory practices that benefit some and asphyxiate others in the process of schooling. We begin our book with a provocative question:

Are we empowered and equipped to have a fighting chance of disrupting the known atrocities that happen under the guise of a "free" public education?

If we are, then why was it a surprise at the start of the pandemic to realize our schools were ill-prepared to address the racial, social, and economic disparities that continue to crush our human spirit? "We cannot afford to wallow in our discomfort regarding issues of race and equity" (Simmons, 2019).

Through the widespread coverage of human stories, statistics, and current realities, we are recognizing and acknowledging that something must change. This unveiling has confirmed that the current crisis of inequity in communities has less to do with the symptoms—which include lack of materials, inconsistent resources, the digital abyss, unattended children, food insecurities, homelessness, unprepared teachers and families, frustrated parents, disengaged students, and school closures—than with the larger problem: a system that lacks collective accountability for being our "brother's keeper."

Schools may be physically safe, have updated resources, be in the "best neighborhoods," and be aesthetically appealing with all of the appropriate building codes to be structurally sound, but they are void of the emotional safety that is needed for students and educators to flourish as individuals who are valued, seen, heard, validated, loved, understood, and cared for in the school community. Billions of Title I funds have been spent in the interest of ensuring that resources are distributed in an equal manner to our schools. However, equality isn't the same as equity. Equality is about distributing resources so that everyone has the same, whereas equity is about providing people with what they need.

Too often in schools, we confuse these two terms and use them synonymously. We have taken steps in our journey toward equality in schools. The *Brown v. Board of Education* decision that overturned the "separate but equal" doctrine of the Jim Crow era and launched a movement to desegregate our schools was a monumental turning point that changed the educational trajectory for millions of US students. Despite this historic precedent, the large gaps and disparities in education that we have alluded to still exist. Some might argue that *Brown* applied a "technical fix" to an adaptive challenge (Heifetz, Grashow, & Linsky, 2009). It has also been stated that desegregation had a destructive impact on the careers and livelihood of many talented Black American educators. As excellent as Black educators were, they were never viewed as good enough.

In 1970 and beyond, America settled for a quiet kind of desegregation compromise between advocates for integration and defenders of segregation that allowed black bodies into white schools, but failed to fully address the actual educational interests of black children. Unreprimanded by a federal government that was no longer committed to full equality but just needed the language of equality for international standing, southern school boards that were opposed to integration fired black teachers and hired white teachers in their place. They closed black schools or demoted them to middle or elementary schools. Because white school boards seemed to believe that black principals did not have the educational capacity to run a school, especially a school in which they would supervise white teachers and oversee the education of white children, black principals were often forced to forfeit their leadership positions. (ASCD, 2019)

Equality is not enough; we desire equity. They sound similar but result in dramatic disparities for BIPOC. Equality is giving everybody the same things. Equity, in contrast, is giving individuals what they need to survive and thrive in our society.

Figure 0.1 depicts dimensions of power, privilege, and oppression. You will notice that privilege and power rests with identities above the dotted line, while systems of oppression are directed at those identities below the line. As a result of the systems of power, privilege, and oppression, some individuals and communities will always be positioned to thrive. Others will only survive, and in some instances, actually perish.

 Shared Experience

Questions to Consider

1. Define dimensions of power and privilege based on the image in Figure 0.1.

2. Define dimensions of oppression based on the image in Figure 0.1.

3. Is this an accurate depiction of dimensions of power and privilege and dimensions of oppression?

4. How do dimensions of power and privilege show up in your organization?

5. How do dimensions of oppression show up in your organization?

FIGURE 0.1   Dimensions of Power, Privilege, and Oppression

Dimensions of Power Privilege

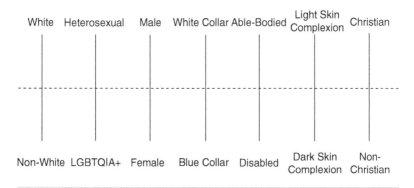

Source: Adapted from Race Matters Institute (2014).

Dimensions of Oppression

DIMENSIONS OF POWER AND PRIVILEGE	DIMENSIONS OF OPPRESSION
white	non-white
heterosexual	LBGTQIA+
male	female
white collar	blue collar
able-bodied	disabled
light skin complexion	dark skin complexion
citizen	non-citizen
Christian	non-Christian
traditional family	nontraditional family
never incarcerated	incarcerated
literate	illiterate
English as a first language	English as an additional language
below average or average weight	above average weight
middle to high income	low to no income
old/older	young

Source: Adapted from Race Matters Institute (2014).

As a result of the systems of power, privilege, and oppression, some individuals and communities will always be positioned to thrive. Others will only survive, and in some instances, actually perish.

Should we settle for the equality provisions of desegregation legislation? In other words, should we applaud the mere fact that we have access to programs that were once only available to white students? Should we commend the aesthetics of physical school environments that are appealing to the eye? Should we praise the fact that, at least in some schools, digital technologies are in the hands of our learners? Should we extol that schools hire multilingual educators? Civil rights legislation like *Brown* has done some good, but after more than 60 years of de facto segregation and countless other barriers to access for BIPOC students, we must conclude it is not enough. It does not address the specific systems of oppression and societal disparities that get in the way of a quality education and enhanced opportunities in life. "The route to achieving equity will not be accomplished through treating everyone equally," says the Race Matters Institute (2014). "It will be achieved by treating everyone equitably, or justly according to their circumstances."

Bryan Stevenson has said the great evil of American slavery wasn't limited to the involuntary servitude that began more than 400 years ago; "it was the fiction that Black people aren't as good as white people, and aren't the equals of white people, and are less evolved, less human, less capable, less worthy, less deserving than white people" (Chotiner, 2020). How does this show up in our schools? In our experiences, we see systems of oppression in school communities across America. There are a multitude of examples including inferior facilities, lack of equitable funding, underprepared educators, curriculum mismatches, and limited extracurriculars and student services. On an even greater scale, we have seen that too few students have been nourished by rigorous and relevant instruction and assessments. Such intellectual malnourishment all too often results in emotionally and physically depleted members of our learning communities. However, despite these formidable obstacles, we have no doubt that the pursuit of educational equity is still worth the effort. But, before taking hold of this challenge, ask yourself, *What will it take and who will get it done?*

Although we are grateful for the impactful and important steps that have been taken to transform and change an educational system that still does not recognize or acknowledge the daily pains and oppressions that are experienced by people of color, we must also ask ourselves, *are these steps enough*? We have a long road ahead of us and an urgency to get to our destination. If we truly share a collective commitment to

 Jot Thought

The Pursuit of Educational Equity

In the graphic organizer below, respond to the question, What will it take?

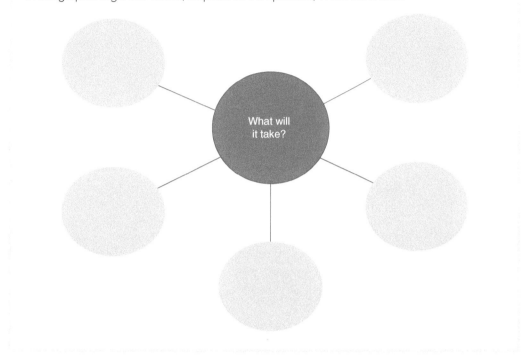

economic, social, and racial justice in our communities, we must conclude that such steps have been insufficient.

In this book, we will identify a learning community that is built upon shared accountability, in which truths are explored and validated and individual cultural experiences are valued through a process called collective equity. The ultimate objective of collective equity is to catalyze the members of the learning community around the work of repairing the damage that has been caused by inequitable systems across generations and create conditions in which we all can thrive on our own terms.

Our Why, Our Conviction, Our Movement

Our (Sonja and Nicole's) heads, hearts, and hands have been connected for more than 20 years and it was unknown to both of us. When our paths crossed in 2017, our gifts collided. We quickly realized that it was our destiny to tell the story of our journey toward creating a better world for ourselves, the young people that we serve, and all humankind. This book is a representation of our newfound simultaneous truths as leaders of equity. Sonja, a social worker, teacher, principal, K–12 district leader in a Southern urban community, a consultant and a director of professional learning for a global solution provider, *embraces communal and collective ways of engaging, empowering, and motivating others for the betterment of all people.* Similarly, Nicole, a teacher, principal, K–12 district leader in a Midwestern urban community, educational consulting business owner, and professional consultant for a global solution provider, *cultivates collaborative atmospheres and contributes to the uplifting of individual voices and communities so that they are empowered and inspired to show up without giving up.*

This work has been burning within us for more than two decades in personal, professional, organizational, and societal levels of engagement. This fire is now ignited and can no longer be contained. There is a sense of urgency (and also sadness) during these tumultuous and destructive times in our world's history. Yet, it has invigorated us to light the darkness of disparities that have plagued our schools throughout centuries, especially for marginalized, ignored, and underserved members of society.

In coming together, we realized that we are more alike than we are different in our philosophy and the ways in which we engage and view the world. And our shared truths revealed that we believe the following:

- Our collective strength and courage gives us the resilience to interrupt the barriers and the beasts of racial and cultural inequities in organizations

- Humility is fundamental in building thriving learning communities that fulfill the promises of equity for all

- A shared sense of accountability for dismantling systems and structures of oppression is created through a Collective Equity Framework

What Is Collective Equity?

Collective refers to collaborative actions, relational interdependence, shared wisdom, and common ambitions. A collective is a group that prioritizes the good of the society over the welfare of the individual. *Equity* refers to teaching, learning, leading, and convening so that biases and inequities are addressed, educational disparities are reduced and eliminated, and policies and practices meet the needs of the members of the learning community, to ensure educational excellence.

Collective equity is a shared responsibility for the social, cultural, academic, and emotional fortification of students and adults that enables everyone to achieve their goals and aspirations on their own terms. It addresses systemic barriers, historic racism, educational disparities, and levels of oppression by fostering culturally fortifying experiences (see Figure 0.2).

How does collective equity show up in our learning communities? We must be vulnerable, take risks, and cultivate an environment of safety to experiment with new or unfamiliar practices, in order to demonstrate relational trust. Relational trust creates the pathway for the community to display a cultural humility that rests upon self- and social awareness, exploration and deep reflection, and the appreciation of diverse perspectives that offer grace. There is a focus on being proactive: considering what is needed before there is a need. These intertwined actions create a natural lift for the entire community that is normalized throughout the organization. It is the culture of the way we collectively show up! When a group works together to elevate and enhance positive outcomes for the learning community, guided by a shared motivation to achieve educational equity, we look beyond our own self-interest and become accountable to one another.

Figure 0.2   What Collective Equity Is and Is Not

WHAT COLLECTIVE EQUITY IS	WHAT COLLECTIVE EQUITY IS NOT
Speaking up for equity, identifying opportunity gaps, and taking ownership for equity transformation	Relying solely on our existing mental models that shape our expectations and efficacy in removing equity barriers
Sharing accountability for disrupting educational disparities that we identify in our organizational system, structures, and practices	Personal accountability for dismantling inequities
Challenging the deficit thinking that exist and replacing it with asset-based actions	Normalizing biased behaviors, language, and practices
Embracing the diverse cultural representations of the members of our learning community	Believing that the members of the learning community must conform to the "way of school"
Building partnerships with families and other members of the community based on shared interests	Designing traditional parent-student activities without including the voices of all members of the community
Cultivating opportunities to accelerate learning by removing barriers that produce learning gaps	Remediating learning by focusing on the gaps and not the strengths of the students

Coming Together

Commitment to Cultural Contributions to the Organization

If you have come here to help me you are wasting your time, but if you have come here because your liberation is bound up with mine, then let us work together.

—Lila Watson

When educators come together, sharing a laser-like focus on diminishing the negative experiences and outcomes of far too many students in our educational system, the results can be powerful. Cultural diversity has steadily increased in the United States and thus in our schools. Since 2014, the majority of students in our public schools have been non-white. Our students enter our classrooms with a rich array of identities including race, gender identity, sexual orientation, social class, religion, cognitive ability, language proficiency, physical ability, and family structure. These dimensions of identity can have a significant impact on how our students (and staff) are seen and how they are received by educators who serve them. When we intentionally understand, honor, and celebrate the dimensions of identity, we can impact teaching, leading, and learning for all.

Coming Together Through Our Shared Truth

Coming together and focusing on equity creates a pathway for effective communication and action. To begin, the members of the learning community must have a shared sense of purpose and desired outcomes. This is accomplished by co-constructing working agreements and protocols that bolster shared truths. **Shared truths** are behaviors, beliefs, values, and realities that are agreed upon across an organization. Creating shared truths requires us to develop a common language, foster a community of trust, be authentic, and honor **equity in voice**. The following are examples of shared truths:

- We believe that teaching is hard work, and we have what it takes to reach and teach all learners

- We believe that our purpose as teachers is to ensure that every student experiences academic success

- We believe that a community learns together

- We believe that impact happens when we update, unlearn, reconsider, and refine

At the same time, shared truths must never negate our unique identities and backgrounds. Being authentic means embodying sincerity that is congruent with our beliefs and value system and supports positive relationships. When we come together to focus on equity in organizations, we commit to developing shared beliefs and values that also honor varying lenses of difference and one another's cultures. Although we value individual contributions to the group's efforts, our collective motivation to create equitable opportunities for learning is driven by cooperative experiences and shared resources and workloads, rather than individualistic achievement and working in silos.

Reimagining schooling through a collectivist lens takes effort because so much of our current system is grounded in principles of individualism and competition. Yet when we consider that many of our students are products of collectivist (rather than individualist) cultures (Hammond, 2015), it stands to reason that the adults in our school communities should practice and model cooperative relationships.

These cooperative relationships depend upon collaborative structures for learning and decision making that are grounded in relational interdependence (Hofstede, 1980). Again, replacing deeply ingrained competitive values and behavior takes work; however, an impetus for forming a collective is the group's commitment to shared wisdom, common ambitions, and a willingness to embrace inclusivity. These actions emphasize the importance of relationships and working cooperatively in collaborative spaces that are culturally inviting.

Think of this learning process as a continuum. As we progress along the continuum toward a higher degree of interdependence, we develop a greater awareness of our own cultural identity, as well as those of others, in a manner that values individual differences and supports collaboration.

The will to understand and display curiosity about others provides the on-ramp into safe spaces of interacting as we become a collective and meet intended group outcomes. In schools, this translates to collective equity. **Collective equity** is a shared responsibility for the social, cultural, academic, and emotional fortification of students and adults that enables learners to achieve their goals and aspirations on their own terms. It addresses systemic barriers, historic racism, educational disparities, and levels of oppression by fostering culturally fortifying experiences.

How do groups make decisions, problem-solve, and create instructional plans with a lens on equity? By establishing **enabling conditions**, which serve as connective tissue to position learning communities to focus on collective equity:

- removing barriers that impede growth

- generating open communication

- creating relational trust

- enacting high levels of engagement

- providing equitable opportunities and resources for each learner's (student, educator, parent) success

These enabling conditions provide opportunities to engage at all three levels: cognitive, emotional, and behavioral. We do this both internally (with ourselves) and externally (with others). Figure 1.1 provides examples of collective equity in practice.

FIGURE 1.1　Collective Equity

ENABLING CONDITIONS	WHAT DOES THIS LOOK LIKE IN PRACTICE?
Removing barriers that impede growth	• Providing access and exposure to relevance and rigor in instruction • Courageously calling out inequities that exist in the system and acting upon them
Generating open communication	• Defining equity to question practices of existing educational disparities in all modes of communication • Providing feedback and coaching as we unlearn, update, refine, and reconsider our ways of being • Listening to others and their perspectives and providing opportunities of equity of voice

(Continued)

FIGURE 1.1 (Continued)

ENABLING CONDITIONS	WHAT DOES THIS LOOK LIKE IN PRACTICE?
Creating relational trust	• Cultivating structures of mutual respect by acknowledging and valuing that everyone has cultural differences
	• Designing opportunities in which members feel safe, brave, affirmed, and protected when sharing their individual insights and beliefs about topics of equity
	• Disrupting the status quo of siloed equity work and fostering a culture of collectivism
Enacting high levels of engagement	• Focusing on the three levels of engagement (behavioral, cognitive, and emotional) to tap into the individual and collective strengths of members of the learning community
	• Building equity skills, knowledge, and stamina through engagement activities such as book studies, affinity group discussions, article analysis, viewing TEDx talks, and highlighting one's lived experiences
Providing equitable opportunities and resources for each learner's (student, educator, parent) success	• Inviting and welcoming parents based on their interests and specific needs that have been voiced by them
	• Strengthening classroom practices to include affirming cultural connections, centering on individual and collective identities while engaging in topics that are meaningful to them
	• Affirming and appreciating staff for their educational knowledge, instructional input, schoolwide contributions, and cultural representations by elevating their voices and creating the conditions for increased engagement

Working Together

Working together in schools has become a cultural norm. **Culture** is the traditions, values, and beliefs that make up an organization and norms are the written or unwritten rules for how we engage with each other. However, working together was not always a part of educational culture. In the past, educators were accustomed to working in isolation with little time carved out for collaboration. The term *professional learning community* (PLC) first emerged among researchers as early as the 1960s to counter the phenomenon of teachers working in isolation. In the late 1980s and early 1990s, the research on deprivatizing practice addressed how to generate PLCs and the benefits of educators having a common time to learn together. This research concluded that, when done right, working together in a PLC or collaborative community benefits teachers as well as students.

Have PLCs lived up to their promise? Michael Fullan (2020) reports that interest in PLCs has moved beyond the "whisper" of researchers to a growing "rallying cry" among practitioners. Teacher team meetings are now ubiquitous fixtures of schools across the nation. However, Fullan also cautions that the term *PLC* has traveled faster than the concept, and many schools are engaged in superficial activities under the banner of PLC that will have little effect on student achievement.

What does "working together" look like in your organization? Some of us have participated in meetings with very structured agendas (often written by someone not participating in the meeting) calling for deliverables from the group. Typically, such endeavors are framed by the lens of accountability and are rarely informed by shared goals, shared wisdom, or levels of interdependence. This isn't very surprising, especially when someone outside the group determines the group's agenda. In other instances, team meetings have an identified leader who is seeking information from team members. In such cases, the members rarely collaborate; instead, they work together to complete a list of tasks. Such task orientation is also indicative of individualist cultures in which product invariably supersedes process.

Our experience over more than two decades as educational leaders and consultants has shown us that the definition of "working together" is rooted in a tradition of *what* we do as individuals, rather than in *how* to focus and drive impactful decisions that result in thriving communities of learning. Merely working together has yet to consistently exert a powerful impact on student learning as it was intended. For us, this is regrettable considering the countless hours, policies, practices, procedures, professional development, and value that have gone into carving out this time for educators.

Coming Together to Work Together

By now, it should be clear that simply "working together" is not the same as "coming together." Collectivist cultures come together "for the good of many" to achieve a common goal (Hofstede, 1980). When focusing on the good of all, we focus on equity. In collectivist cultures, integrated groups perceive their interdependence and obligations to the community as unstated norms. In most schools, the PLCs are groups of educators *working* together. Most researchers, as well as practitioners, would agree that PLCs should create a collective process whereby educators engage in the following:

- Achieving a clear, common purpose for student learning

- Creating a collaborative culture to achieve the purpose

- Taking collective—rather than individual—responsibility for the learning of all students

- Coming together with relentless advocacy, efficacy, agency, and ownership for learning

 Jot Thought

Relentlessly Coming Together in PLCs

With members of your learning community, identify ways in which advocacy, efficacy, agency, and ownership are evident in your PLCs.

COLLECTIVE ACTIONS FOR COMING TOGETHER IN PLCs	HOW DO THESE COLLECTIVE ACTIONS SHOW UP IN YOUR PLCs?
Advocacy	
Efficacy	
Agency	
Ownership	

 Available for download from resources.corwin.com/CollectiveEquity

Teams that come together to focus on historical educational disparities, current inequities, and opportunity gaps share momentum to fulfill the promise of equity. In our consulting work coaching teams and delivering professional development, we emphasize an overarching focus on equity. Equity-focused PLCs are spaces where members identify and apply specific evidence-based practices that affirm the cultural connections and backgrounds of every student. Such teams strive to incorporate culturally fortifying practices that enhance the cognition, engagement, and learning of all students. Culturally fortifying practices are shared and implemented among all the members of the learning community. In addition, the team interrogates the cultural relevance of curriculum, instruction, and assessments in the interest of improving student engagement and closing instructional gaps. As PLCs confront the brutal facts of our quantitative and qualitative data and the current realities faced by students and their families, we evolve in our practice and are committed to continuously asking, "Who benefited and who did not?" (Fisher, Frey, Almarode, Flories, & Nagel, 2019).

Although these are all laudable pursuits, there is one critical aspect of the process that is missing: *understanding*. More specifically, how can we take a collective approach to this work if we don't know or leverage the *cultural* dimensions of working as a collective? Without an understanding of the dynamics of cultural differences between ourselves, our colleagues, our students, and members of our greater community, we cannot come together as a collective or focus on the learning of all students.

More plainly stated, you cannot be a quilt with just one square.

In the remainder of this chapter, we will highlight how understanding ourselves and each other when considering the dimensions of identity and levels of culture is foundational to creating collective equity in our learning communities.

Connecting Dimensions of Identity

What impedes the interlacing of cultures? Humans long for connections, attachments, and relationships, but through societal structures that are rooted in individualist ways of making meaning (e.g., the US Constitution, the three branches of government, the Declaration of Independence, the Bill of Rights, the Pledge of Allegiance, and unwritten [Eurocentric] cultural norms), we are forced into independence, silos, and autonomy rather than interdependence. A relentless focus on competitiveness prevents the community from coming together by creating structures where we only work together but never come together. This dismantles our opportunity to produce and fortify outcomes that have a positive impact for everyone.

To achieve the vision of coming together, we must first engage in personal cultural awareness by unlearning, updating, reconsidering, and refining our knowledge, attitudes, skills, and beliefs in a manner that frees us to deeply engage with colleagues, students, and families. What does this look like and why is it important? Too often we make statements that negatively impact individuals, such as,

- "Good morning ladies and gentlemen."

- "Today boys and girls…"

- "Where are you going on Christmas break?"

- "What did your family have for Thanksgiving dinner?"

- "That is so gay!"

- "You are retarded!"

✎ Jot Thought

Negative Statements

What other statements have you heard that could negatively impact individuals?

_____

_____

_____

_____

FIGURE 1.2   Constrained and Unconstrained Equity

CONSTRAINED EQUITY EXAMPLES	UNCONSTRAINED EQUITY EXAMPLES
There is no need to change because we have come a long way. *(We had a Black president—President Barack Obama)*	There is a desire to expand our knowledge of other cultures and the dimension of identities in order to see the plight of historically marginalized groups of people. *(Approval of state reparations for Black people)*
America is not a racist country. *(All lives matter)*	Awareness of the "isms" that exist for oppressed cultures that are outside of the dominant cultures *(Pride commemorative celebrations for LBGTQIA+ individuals)*
America is a melting pot that embraces everybody. *(Deferred Action for Childhood Arrivals)*	The hiring of Diversity, Equity and Inclusion leaders in all industries *(Walmart, Zoom, Gucci, Amazon, and many school districts across the US)*

In order to evolve to where you embrace cultural differences, you must display *unconstrained equity*. To embody **unconstrained equity,** one must have an openness and capacity to appreciate differences; display a **crisis of consciousness** in which we recognize and own the internal dissonance that comes along with challenges to what we have always known, believed, and valued; and have a personal and ongoing commitment to be better. This requires listening, learning, questioning, reflecting, and collaborating with a deep sense of humility to transform our individualistic ways of working together into collectivist actions where we come together. Unconstrained equity is a lifelong growth process.

In contrast, **constrained equity** is typically performative and has an endpoint at which our growth stops and we are no longer conscious of our blind spots (see Figure 1.2). Constrained equity often ends with the belief that we have progressed to a post-racial society or, as individuals, we have acquired a sufficient degree of cultural competency and "wokeness."

Our crisis of consciousness creates a "knowing-doing gap" in our respect, responsiveness, and relationships within our collaborative communities. This gap exists between what we know versus what we should or choose to take immediate action on. For some (most significantly, those who are members of the dominant majority), the dimensions of identity that show up in these communities are an unwanted intrusion. Consider the norm of so-called colorblindness ("I don't see color"). Unfortunately, it is still a reality in many of our schools and organizations, and one that invalidates a person's sense of being, belonging, and becoming. When you don't see color, you don't know the fullness of that person, ignoring who they are and impacting the rich opportunities of being in a collective. When we don't feel seen or included, we are unable to come together; therefore, the team is not a collective.

There are multiple facets of identity that are integral to our sense of belonging and inclusivity. If we do not know ourselves, how can we come together to achieve our common goals? In our schools and our pluralistic society as a whole, our lives are impacted by intersectionalities of identities: race, gender identity, social class, sexual orientation, language, religious affiliation, age, physical ability, gender expression, and ethnicity, to name a few. The theory of intersectionality posits that there are systems in society that give some people advantages over others based upon their intersecting identities (Crenshaw, 1989). The intersections of aspects of identity may create modes of discrimination and privilege. Facets of identity are linked to corresponding systems of oppression (e.g., racism, sexism, heteronormativity, cisnormativity) that perpetuate inequities.

Figure 1.3 is a representation of the dimensions of identity, which include intersectionalities that make up who we are as individuals. When we cultivate an understanding of the dimensions of identity we not only become more self-aware, but we increase our understanding and appreciation of others' identities. This understanding impacts and influences who we are as professionals.

When we embrace who *we* are, we can recognize the multi-dimensional identities of others. The result—increased group harmony—makes us more effective as a collective. Returning to our quilt metaphor, dimensions of identity can be individually represented as quilt squares. In

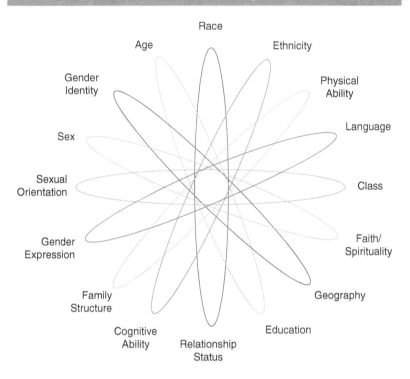

FIGURE 1.3   The Dimensions of Identity

order to become a collectivist community, each square must be inter-woven with threads of social fusion: creativity, compassion, communi-cation, collaboration, courage, and conscious curiosity about ourselves and others. Considering the intersectionalities of the dimensions of identity increases understanding of the privilege, power, and oppres-sion that hinder individuals and communities from appearing in the fullness of who they are. As we reflect on our own experiences of how we enter personal, professional, and societal spaces, we share with you a glimpse of our world.

Nicole was born in Blythville, Arkansas to a college-educated mother who was married to a military officer. Her mother decided after many years of marriage that she could no longer be married. She became a divorced mother. When Nicole and her family moved to Gary, Indi-ana it was a life of joy, comfort, and pain. For Nicole, this dichotomy of emotions and experiences was born out of her intersectionality of physical health and the family dynamics. A genetic disorder (sickle cell anemia) created a world where hospitalizations were normal for Nicole. Nicole also became well aware of the judgments and mental models that surfaced in her interactions with others—particularly the belief that her family was not good enough for a community filled with two-parent homes. As an adult, Nicole navigates and negotiates spaces as a Black woman with a debilitating illness who also holds a PhD. Because of these intersectionalities, she is forced to constantly survey whether she can show up in the fullness of who she is.

Sonja was born in Anderson, South Carolina and enjoyed the laughter and love that her family and other children gave to her at a very young age. As a result of desegregation, she landed in an all-white elementary school at the ripe age of 6. A Black child who was taught the value of an education from a very early age by grandparents, parents, aunts and uncles, all of whom had graduated from college, she entered this space with excitement and curiosity about the world around her. Although she was excited and curious, she faced the ugliness of racism in the South on the very first day of school when none of the other children even called her name, nor did the teacher acknowledge her. Think about it: How does one who grew up in a world where education is valued as a gift enter into another world where, because of her race, she is no longer afforded that gift? As an adult, Sonja has realized that in many spaces, being educated and Black is not seen and valued as a gift. In this case, the intersections of Sonja's Blackness with her status as a well-educated American (she holds a doctoral degree) have had a significant impact on how she shows up in the world.

After completing the engagement activity below, consider how each dimension might bring benefits and burdens for Nicole and Sonja.

🖊 Jot Thought

Personal Awareness

Reflect upon the intersectionalities that are meaningful for you. Be real in this space as you explore past and present realities of who you are.

	As a child, which of the following dimensions of identity were pronounced for you?	As an adult, which of the following dimensions of identity are pronounced for you?	As an educator, which of the following dimensions of identity are pronounced for you?	Which ones are the most important to you now?	Which ones do you believe others typically notice about you?	Which ones impact your existence the most in society?
AGE						
APPEARANCE						

(Continued)

(Continued)

	As a child, which of the following dimensions of identity were pronounced for you?	As an adult, which of the following dimensions of identity are pronounced for you?	As an educator, which of the following dimensions of identity are pronounced for you?	Which ones are the most important to you now?	Which ones do you believe others typically notice about you?	Which ones impact your existence the most in society?
BODY IMAGE						
COGNITIVE ABILITY						
DIALECT						
EDUCATION						
ETHNICITY						
FAMILY STRUCTURE						
GENDER EXPRESSION						
GENDER IDENTITY						
GEOGRAPHIC LOCATION						
HEALTH STATUS						
IMMIGRANT STATUS						
INDIGENOUS ORIGIN						
LANGUAGE						
MENTAL HEALTH STATUS						
NATIONALITY						
PARENTAL STATUS						
PHYSICAL ABILITY						
PROFESSIONAL STATUS						
RACE						
RELATIONSHIP STATUS						
RELIGION/ SPIRITUALITY						
SEXUAL ORIENTATION						

SKIN COMPLEXION	
SOCIOECONOMIC STATUS	
STATURE	
OTHER	

Which dimensions of identity have been most prevalent throughout your life?

_____

_____

_____

_____

_____

Do the members of the collective share your dimensions of identity? How so?

_____

_____

_____

_____

_____

What did you experience from this engagement activity?

_____

_____

_____

_____

_____

online resources ▸ Available for download from resources.corwin.com/CollectiveEquity

Community Agreements and Equity Fatigue

Below are examples of how three schools approached the practice of building collective equity by celebrating dimensions of identity.

Field Examples of Building Collective Equity by Celebrating Dimensions of Identity

On the opening day of school at Melton City Elementary School, the staff was invited to participate in a group activity: decorating squares of a quilt to represent their personal and/or professional identities. Nancy Larson, the principal, invited staff members to tell their stories through visual imagery on their personalized squares. They then assembled the squares in a manner that symbolized who they were as a community. This quilt hung in the cafeteria and was a constant reminder to celebrate warmth, unity, and the sense of belonging of each team member.

Broad Street High School celebrates the staff by sharing "I Am From" poems. This activity embraces each member of the team through storytelling and sharing life experiences from a dimension of culture. This engagement strategy allows staff to express themselves as individuals but, at the same time, promotes an understanding that we are more alike than we are different. Time is set aside for each member to craft their "I Am From" poem using the George Ella Lyon poem "Where I'm From" as a template. Participants add layers of complexity and vulnerability as they share reflections from their life experiences. Bill Maxi and the administrative team create space for staff members to share their poems with one another. This opens the door for connections, appreciation of each other's creativity, and enhanced cultural awareness. One teacher said, "This was a powerful activity and gave me insight on my co-workers that will be an imprint in my head and heart. I have a new found level of the value of really knowing my colleagues."

Harper Middle School engages staff in a show and tell using the activity "Cultural Brown Bag." In this activity, staff members are asked to bring an item that reflects their culture. This activity provides a perfect way for coworkers to get to know each other on a deeper level. Staff have brought items from childhood, heirlooms from relatives, photographs, items of clothing, and books and items that are sentimental and valued by the individuals who are sharing aspects of their culture. It is a great way to open up conversations and questions about our colleagues in order to get to know them better.

Shared Experience

Create a social fusion activity representing members of the learning community coming together to celebrate dimensions of identity (e.g., quilt, "I am" poetry, cultural brown bag).

SOCIAL FUSION ENGAGEMENT

 Available for download from resources.corwin.com/CollectiveEquity

The three examples above were drawn from communities that have agreements for how they work, share experiences, and come together. **Community agreements** are protocols or ground rules for guiding conversations and engagement strategies focusing on cultural awareness. Skilled facilitators lead staff members through a process of identifying the guidelines and conditions necessary for full engagement. These agreements open the door to productive conversations about personal and complex issues that we generally avoid in a working environment and can disrupt the crisis of consciousness. As the development of community agreements evolve within the collective, we must cultivate self-awareness and surround ourselves with the support of other members in the community. This is complex work requiring hypervigilance to tap into all aspects of our being. Once we decide to do this work, there is no resting. Equity is a state of being. It is not something that we do; it is who we are. This journey is known to evoke an emotional impact that at times causes feelings of hopelessness, despair, frustration, shame, anger, exhaustion, and blame. As we enter into this work and guide each other on our journey toward equity, we must attend to ourselves because *equity fatigue* is real. This term has been around for years, but it's often just used when people are tired of talking about equity. *Equity fatigue is more than that.* It is a condition of physical and mental exhaustion, and this is something many leaders of color face because inequity is relentless.

While our white colleagues may be able to walk away if they get tired of these conversations, we can't take a break; we can't walk away; we will always be of color. The world will always see us as "of color," even when it claims to be "color-blind." (Le, 2017)

While in the field we have noticed that educators of color are experiencing a reckoning as they are chosen to carry the torch for this work, sometimes by choice and other times by the mere fact that they are thought to be the spokesperson for oppressed groups because of their race. Although this can be cathartic and healing, it is also emotionally depleting.

> Caring for myself is not self-indulgence, it is self-preservation, and that is an act of political warfare.
>
> —Audre Lorde

Equity fatigue can occur in each of us on our journey toward equity. We must be reflective and self-aware in order to remain on the journey for the long haul. Transformation will not happen overnight. Equity work is exhausting but also rewarding and, as equity champions, we must take care of ourselves. One way is through cultivating a relationship with an equity commitment partner who will serve as a confidant and provide external support, a listening ear, shared passion, reflective feedback, a strength-based mindset, and reciprocity of trust and respect for the relationship. In order to do this work, we need each other to survive and thrive.

Jot Thought

My Equity Commitment Partner

In the chart below, identify your equity commitment partner and what that connection will entail.

My equity commitment partner is	
I need the following from my partner	↕ _____ ↕ _____ ↕ _____ ↕ _____ ↕ _____
We will check in	↕ daily ↕ two times per week ↕ three times per week ↕ bi-weekly ↕ monthly

Community agreements are one step toward precluding the occurrence of equity fatigue in that they help to promote healthy relationships and interactions across the community. When we engage in co-constructing such agreements, we enter into a process driven by relationships and a commitment to the learning community. These agreements require trust, vulnerability, openness, safety, and bravery. A healthy culture within the learning community is foundational for sustainability. This happens when relationships are pure, authentic, and sincere. Community agreements shape how the group moves into spaces of high trust and low fear (Howard, 2015). For communities to navigate their journey to collective equity, there must be agreements that shape brave, inclusive, and supportive interactions and are grounded in their *shared truths.*

Jot Thought

Examples of Community Agreements

COMMUNITY AGREEMENT	SHARED MEANING
Mutual respect	Respecting the values, ideas. and beliefs of others; not imposing our own onto others
Active listening	Fully concentrating on what is being said rather than just passively "hearing" the message of the speaker, in order to fully understand the message, comprehend the information, and respond thoughtfully
Right to pass	The right to not participate in the sharing and instead sit quietly listening to the interactions
Trust intent/name impact	Assuming the "good will" of others and identifying the personal emotional charge on oneself based upon others' actions
Stay engaged (emotionally, physically, and cognitively)	Participating by exhibiting curiosity about the topics, posing questions, and seeking feedback
Take care of yourself (emotionally, physically, and cognitively)	Monitoring what you need and managing your stress from the actions of others

Tap into your inner experience: what other agreements might be added?

_____

_____

_____

_____

_____

online resources ☞ Available for download from resources.corwin.com/CollectiveEquity

Shared Experience

Using the agreements each group member added to the previous exercise, create a set of shared community agreements. A member of the group takes the lead by asking the other members to share out their individual examples through a process of synthesis and agreement. Once you have identified the common set, post them and review them prior to each time you "come together" as a collective.

SHARED COMMUNITY AGREEMENTS

 Available for download from resources.corwin.com/CollectiveEquity

Coming Together Using a Collective Equity Framework

School cultures aren't formed in a vacuum. Our schools are continually influenced by general trends, events, and actions of our society, most notably the overarching policies that are enacted in the sociopolitical arena. Author/consultant Gary Howard (2015) developed a useful framework called Levels of Engagement, shown in Figure 1.4.

FIGURE 1.4   Gary Howard's Levels of Engagement

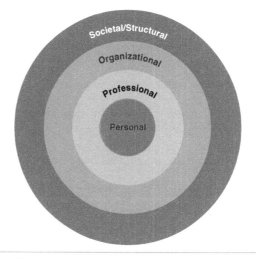

Source: Reprinted from Howard (2015).

Much of what we have experienced as "school reform" has been based on a top-down model, driven by accountability and compliance and informed by the societal/structural level. Howard (2015) refers to such carrot-and-stick efforts as "market-driven," in direct contrast to the collectivist ways of being that are at the heart of this book. After enduring decades of such policies and practices one thing remains clear: we've done little to close the opportunity gaps that have created barriers to the success of historically marginalized groups, including students of color and those living in low-income households.

Rather than a top-down model in which our actions and decisions are driven by the outer ring of the circle in Figure 1.4, we propose that the levels of engagement are interdependent, thereby creating the Collective Equity Framework (Figure 1.5). Moreover, the evolution of the collective begins with personal consciousness—the inner circle. If we do not have an understanding of our own culture and how it informs our beliefs and values, we are not equipped to evolve with others in our professional practice in a manner that creates equitable learning experiences. We must collectively agree to value preservation of identity, honor differences, and honor individual assets. This is not antithetical to coming together as a collective. Rather than thinking of the collective as a melting pot, think back to our quilt metaphor in which each square maintains its own uniqueness and beauty, but together they form a unified work of artistry. Coming together as a collective is a relational process of respecting, honoring, and learning from one another using a lens of difference. Again, what makes it a collective is that we catalyze around the greater good. Changing systems requires changing people, and changing people requires changing systems (Fullan, 2009). In contrast to the top-down model, our enabling conditions move from the inside out, requiring *collective engagement* among everyone in the organization. As we gain new self-understanding and engage with one another in the collective, we gain greater insight into how our actions and decisions influence not only our professional practice but our organizations and society as a whole.

Equity Pathways and Equity Pavers

When we come together as learners, we become more adept at identifying how our decisions and actions can be pathways or barriers to equity. An *equity pathway* is a roadmap for equitable transformations that addresses educational disparities. It is a process

FIGURE 1.5   The Collective Equity Framework

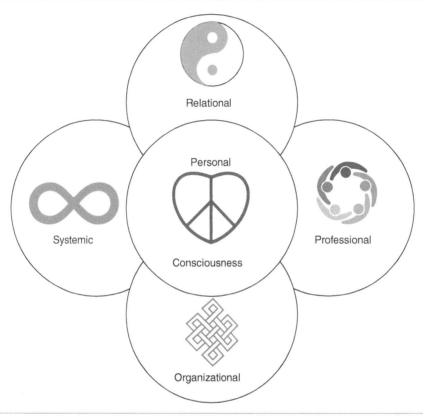

Image Source: pixabay.com/GDJ, pixabay.com/dinarpoz, pixabay.com/openclipart-vectors, istock.com/oleskii arseniuk, istock.com/DESKCUBE

for acquiring knowledge, building skills, shaping attitudes, and strengthening stamina for collective actions to diminish inequities in our learning community. Below are examples of equity pathways that address specific inequities in our schools:

- Creating culturally fortifying environments

- Cultivating anti-racist education

- Building cultural literacy of learning community members

- Enhancing equity partnerships with families and community members

- Designing culturally relevant instruction

- Fostering equitable and inclusive working environments

As we travel toward equitable transformations, we strive to identify and validate where people are on the journey. Transforming schools into equitable environments can only be achieved if the members of the learning community increase their equity knowledge, attitudes, and skills. This is accomplished using techniques we call *equity pavers*. An equity paver is a scaffold, or step along our equity pathway, that helps us identify the prior knowledge, attitudes, and skills of the learning community. It also describes concrete action steps that we can take to realize our desired outcomes as defined by our pathways. Equity pavers provide entry points that leverage prior knowledge and determine a logical sequence for *creating communities where we all can breathe.*

An equity paver is directly aligned to the specified equity pathway. Pavers help us observe our own growth and monitor our progress toward cultural humility. For example, if your equity pathway is to culturally fortify all the students in the learning community, then your equity pavers (the actions the collective will take) could include the following:

Equity Pathway: Create a culturally fortifying environment

Equity Pavers:

- Book study: *Culturally Responsive Teaching and the Brain* by Zaretta Hammond

- Professional learning on culturally fortifying practices

- Coaching on the implementation of culturally fortifying instructional practices

- Build a culturally fortifying school and classroom library

- Conduct an equity audit

- Engage all staff in DOT inventory (a process used to ensure that every student is known in the learning community. Students names are posted around the room and teachers place dots on names of students where they have a significant relationship. This provides a visualization to making sure every student is known)

- Create a culturally relevant welcome center for families and community members

- Regularly monitor the experiences of the adult members of our learning community (e.g., do we all feel safe in speaking our respective truths?)

- Obtain student feedback on our culturally fortifying practices. How are we actually doing?

The identification of equity pathways and equity pavers provides opportunities to give birth to collective actions for creating equitable learning environments for all. Figure 1.6 illustrates how equity pavers align with the Collective Equity Framework.

FIGURE 1.6   Examples of Equity Pavers Within the Dimensions of the Collective Equity Framework

DIMENSION OF THE COLLECTIVE EQUITY FRAMEWORK	EQUITY PAVERS
Personal	Collective engagement strategies focusing on the following: • dimensions of identity • bias recognition • levels of culture
Relational	Collective engagement strategies focusing on the following: • social fusion activities that create cultural interconnectedness • generosity and kindness toward others • interactions displaying humility
Professional	Professional learning opportunities focusing on the following: • culturally fortifying pedagogy • culturally sustaining leadership • agentic vs. communal dispositions
Organizational	Continuous school improvement actions focusing on the following: • system/school equity data • human development and empowerment • equitable strategic resourcing
Systemic	Sociopolitical actions focusing on the following: • systemic inequities impacting schools • white supremacy and public education • criminalization of students and discipline policies

Understanding the Three Levels of Culture

We have a moral imperative as a relational society to personally, professionally, and organizationally confront who we are as individuals and our relationship to the conditions that enable systemic inequities and oppression. The Collective Equity Framework informs how we interact as individuals and summon the unique assets that we bring into the community, which not only help us know one another as individuals, but also help us understand and appreciate cultures outside of our own. In exploring such differences, we gain greater insight into why we do what we do and what is important to us. Similarly, we learn how our own cultural values and assumptions may differ from others in the learning community.

Sonja and Nicole have had the experience of asking five different people from a school how they would define their school culture and receiving five very different answers. As well, most of our school improvement plans are heavily laden with activities that require us to focus on building a positive school culture and climate. Paradoxically, the objectives very rarely take into account the people who actually make up and create the culture. These are surface-level activities that provide an introduction, but by themselves will not create a culture where everyone feels seen, heard, valued, and validated.

Many of us have participated in superficial events in the interest of "culture building." An example of this is the "international day" ritual that is typically scheduled with little thought given to its objective or any follow-up to the activity. As we wrote this chapter, we reminisced about how we enjoyed the food, snapped our fingers to the music, danced and moved to the rhythms of the cultural expressions, and adorned ourselves with a variety of clothing items that were even called "costumes." (Consider the culturally insensitive implications of even using such a word in this context!) However, did we know any better?

After the day was over, after we cleaned the cafeteria, after we went back to our rooms and offices, nothing about our school culture had changed. One of our reasons for writing this book is the knowledge that educators (ourselves included) may have great intentions, but we don't know what we don't know. If an isolated activity like international day does not create a community of inclusivity, what are schools to do to provide authentic experiences that will build a pluralistic school culture that allows us to connect in ways that extend beyond our one-time "cultural events."

So, what does culture have to do with it? As it turns out, everything. Simply stated, the people in an organization build the culture. We become collectivist around our cultural expressions. Culture is highly nuanced, but fundamentally it operates on three levels: the surface culture, the shallow or intermediate culture, and deep culture (Hammond, 2015, p. 22). We are wired to cognitively operate this way, and because of this, everyone embodies their culture regardless of their specific dimensions of difference. Our culture drives our attitude, actions, and our affirmations for one another and ultimately makes meaning of what happens with us and to us every day.

Surface culture consists of the type of music we listen to, the attire that adorns us, food that we savor, the traditions and stories that we tell, and dancing to the rhythm of cultural expressions. Although it's imperative to understand and embrace these patterns of observable culture, this level has low emotional impact on trust, and low trust impedes relationship building. Other examples of surface culture are hair styles and speaking styles, which often stimulate biases and judgments from the dominant culture. Why are these aspects of surface culture uncelebrated? When we pick and choose the aspects of culture that we are uncomfortable embracing, we choose to not see people. We also choose to decrease the opportunity for us to connect beyond a surface-level, thereby impacting the way we work together and support a healthy, thriving learning community.

Immersive Experience

Read the three narratives below and engage in the **Jot Thought** to tap into your inner experience using the three levels of culture.

Narrative 1: Author Paul Gorski highlights an example of a surface cultural experience.

Taco Night by Paul C. Gorski

I remember the invitations: red text on a white background, the name of the event in a curly bold face surrounded by a crudely drawn piñata, a floppy sombrero, and a dancing cucaracha. A fourth grader that year, I gushed with enthusiasm about these sorts of cultural festivals—the different, the alien, the other—dancing around me, a dash of spice for a child of white flighters. Ms. Manning distributed the invitations in mid-April, providing parents ample time to plan for the event, which occurred the first week of May, on or around Cinco de Mayo.

A few weeks later my parents and I, along with a couple hundred other parents, teachers, students, and administrators, crowded into the cafeteria for Guilford Elementary School's annual Taco Night. The occasion was festive. I admired the colorful decorations, like the papier mâché piñatas designed by fifth-grade classes, then watched my parents try to squeeze themselves into cafeteria-style tables built for eight-year-olds. Sometimes the school hired a Mexican song and dance troupe from a neighboring town. They'd swing and sway and sing and smile and I'd watch, bouncing dutifully to the rhythm, hoping they'd play La Bamba or Oye Como Va so I could sing along, pretending to know the words. If it happened to be somebody's birthday the music teacher would lead us in a lively performance of Cumpleaños Feliz and give the kid some Mexican treats.

¡Olé!

Granted, not a single Mexican or Mexican-American student attended Guildford at the time. However, I do recall Ms. Manning asking Adolfo, a classmate whose family had immigrated from Guatemala, whether the Taco Night tacos were "authentic." He answered with a shrug. Granted, too, there was little educational substance to the evening; I knew no more about Mexico or Mexican-American people upon leaving Taco Night than I did upon arriving. And granted, we never discussed more important concerns like, say, racism faced by Mexican Americans or the long history of U.S. imperialist intervention throughout Latin America. Still, hidden within Taco Night and the simultaneous absence of meaningful curricular attention to Mexicans, Mexican Americans, Chicanx people, or Latinx people more broadly, were three critical and clarifying lessons: (1) Mexican culture is synonymous with tacos; (2) "Mexican" and "Guatemalan" are synonymous and by extension all Latinx people are the same and by further extension all Latinx people are synonymous with tacos (as well as sombreros and dancing cucarachas); and (3) white people love tacos, especially in those hard, crunchy shells, which, I learned later, nobody in Mexico eats.

Thus began my diversity education—my introduction to a clearly identifiable "other." And I could hardly wait until Pizza Night.

✎ Jot Thought

Tap Into Your Inner Experience

What was your Taco Night?

_____

_____

_____

What cultural events have you participated in?

_____

_____

_____

Do you recall any cultural insensitivities?

_____

_____

_____

What was the intent of these events?

_____

_____

_____

What was the impact on others?

_____

_____

_____

What considerations can be made to create a fortifying experience for all?

_____

_____

_____

Shallow culture consists of the unstated norms and unspoken rules that impact our social interactions, such as appropriate touching, rules about eye contact, and our nonverbal ways of interacting. It colors our thoughts around being courteous, such as how to treat adults if you are a child and elders if you are an adult. It is the nucleus of budding friendships and who we choose to spend time with, how we spend time with them, and how we communicate with others or perceive how they communicate with us. "It's at this level of culture that we put into action our deep cultural values. Nonverbal communication that builds rapport and trust between people comes out of shallow culture" (Hammond, 2015).

At this level of culture, we make our decisions about how (or whether) we will come together with our colleagues, parents, students, and community. Coming together is about us identifying the purpose of the learning community and considering the outcomes up front. This includes co-constructing community agreements and protocols that bolster shared truths. At this juncture of creating a school culture, we move into spaces that are often laden with highly charged emotional expressions.

We observe and judge the actions of our colleagues or others in many different ways that can be positive or negative. If the latter, our interactions may be interpreted as disrespectful, hostile, and aggressive. Violations of cultural norms at this level impede trust, force social silos, and can even cause high anxiety and distress. It is our recommendation that when professionals enter this level of building and creating a productive and positive culture, they engage in surface-level activities and create "community agreements" that respectfully consider the intersectionality and awareness of the cultures that make up our beautifully diverse community.

Narrative 2: Author Justin Hauver highlights an example of a shallow cultural experience.

Student Transgressions by Justin Haver

Ms. Regis, the counselor at Redline Middle School, took a deep breath and settled back into her chair as the conference room door softly clicked shut. She glanced at the eighth-grade teachers sitting around the table and felt uncertain about how to begin. In her two decades at Redline, she had never encountered a transgender-questioning student, at least not one who was open about it. Times were changing and she wondered if she could keep up—or if she wanted to. Mr. Guler, a veteran science teacher, saved her the trouble of starting the meeting, "So, what do we do about Keith?" "That's what we're here to figure out," Ms. Regis responded. "I've spoken with his mom"—should she say "her mom"?

Ms. Regis wondered—"and Ms. Carter is at a loss. She has tried talking with Keith and taking away his phone and his XBox. Nothing seems to work. She did make clear that she did not want Keith to be allowed to wear the wig at school and she's going to try to prevent him from posting any more pictures on social media." Last month, Keith had come to school wearing a blond wig and asking to be called "K'Brianna." The results had not been positive for Keith or for his teachers. Other students at Redline had bullied him mercilessly during breakfast even though teachers, somewhat dumbfounded, had tried to intervene. Keith's first period class had been so disrupted by his appearance that Mrs. Thomas, his math teacher, had sent him to the office just to get the class calm. When he refused to take off the wig, he was sent home for violating the school's prohibitions of hats and "provocative clothing." He came back the next day without the wig, claiming that the whole thing was an experiment. "Call me Keith, stupid," he said when students made jokes about "K'Brianna." His teachers continued trying to enforce Redline's anti-bullying policy whenever they heard someone making fun of Keith, but they were left confused by the whole event. Many staff members came from the local community, a very conservative town in the southern United States, and they had no direct experience with transgender issues. Some were also reluctant to defend transgender expressions for personal or religious reasons.

The final level of culture that Hammond (2015) defines is *deep culture*. "Deep culture is what grounds the individual and nourishes his mental health. It is the bedrock of self-concept, group identity, approaches to problem-solving, and decision making (Hammond, 2015, p. 24). At this level, we make unconscious assumptions that govern the way we see the world. Those things we know and hold as our truths are understood and implied without being stated. As an example, if one person makes a statement to another person who remains silent, the silence can be interpreted as agreement or approval. In our current time of social crisis around justice for Black and brown people, we have heard the phrase "silence is an agreement to the ills of our justice system," particularly for facets of our community that have the privilege.

In school organizations where we come together and work together, deep culture governs how we learn new information. This level also has an intense emotional charge, and the mental models we have created for ourselves influence our thoughts and our interpretation of threats and rewards in the environment. In other words, how we see ourselves and how the world views us. At this cultural level, the threats can be deemed microaggressions, which harm the working relationship. Microaggressions are the subtle snubs, inappropriate jokes, and unintentional discrimination against marginalized groups that emotionally disrupt feelings of connectivity and how we do our work. These aggressive acts are expressed as invalidations, insults, and the most destructive, assaults. If we feel that cultural values are being challenged, our brains revert to the fight or flight response—a response that inherently moves us farther away from coming together.

Source: Reprinted from justiceinschools.org. Used with permission.

Jot Thought

Tap Into Your Inner Experience

What was your transgression conversation?

_____

_____

_____

Identify inclusive conversations you have participated in.

_____

_____

_____

Do you recall any cultural insensitivities?

_____

_____

_____

What was the intent of these conversations?

_____

_____

_____

(Continued)

(Continued)

What was the impact on others?

_____

_____

_____

What considerations can be made to create a fortifying experience
for all?

_____

_____

_____

Image Source: istock.com/LeoPatrizi

**Narrative 3: Authors Heather Johnson and Ellis Reid
highlight an example of a deep cultural experience.**

***Politics, Partisanship, and Pedagogy: What Should be
Controversial in the Classroom? by Heather Johnson and
Ellis Reid***

*The 10th-grade social studies team at Northern High School is meet-
ing to identify topics for this year's Power of Persuasion (PoP) assign-
ments, a core element of their curriculum. PoP required students to*

research an issue, critically evaluate it, take a position, and present their arguments to classmates. After agreeing on the Dakota Access Pipeline as their first topic, one teacher proposes the creation of a Muslim registry as another. There seems to be general agreement that the topic is empirically controversial—that is, an active debate in the current political landscape. However, the teachers disagree that a Muslim registry should be treated as an open topic in their school. Just because something is being publicly debated, does that mean it should be? On the one hand, they are a department that is committed to preparing students to be informed and engaged citizens who can think critically about complex issues. On the other hand, some had trouble imagining how an open, balanced debate on a Muslim registry squared with a commitment to democratic ideals of tolerance, equality, and human rights. How had religious discrimination become something that is controversial, not just wrong? Some argue that it is ethically problematic to present both sides. Others argue that it is ethically problematic to present it in an unbalanced way or to avoid it altogether.

Source: Reprinted from justiceinschools.org. Used with permission.

✎ Jot Thought

Tap Into Your Inner Experience

What was your Muslim registry?

_____

_____

_____

What controversial curriculum decisions have you participated in?

_____

_____

_____

Do you recall any cultural insensitivities?

_____

_____

_____

(Continued)

(Continued)

What was the intent of these conversations?

_____

_____

_____

What was the impact on others?

_____

_____

_____

What considerations can be made to create a fortifying experience for all?

_____

_____

_____

Figure 1.7 provides examples of the three levels of cultural representation.

FIGURE 1.7   Levels of Cultural Representation

Surface Culture: Observable patterns Low emotional impact on trust	<ul><li>Speech patterns</li><li>Cooking</li><li>Holidays</li><li>Songs</li><li>Art</li><li>Language</li><li>Music</li><li>Hair styles</li><li>Food</li><li>Clothes</li><li>Dance</li><li>Games</li><li>Drama</li><li>Literature</li><li>Stories</li></ul>

Shallow Culture:

Unspoken rules

High emotional impact on trust

- Concepts of time
- Acceptable food sources
- Personal space
- Eye contact
- Ways of handling emotion
- Nature of relationships
- Tempo of work
- Being honest
- Nonverbal communication
- Theories of wellness & disease
- Child-rearing principles

Deep Culture:

Collective unconscious (beliefs & norms)

Intense emotional impact on trust

- Decision making
- Concepts of self
- World view
- Definitions of kinship & group identity
- Cosmology (how the world began)
- Spirituality & concept of a higher power
- Relationship to nature and animals
- Preferences for completion or cooperation
- Notion of fairness

Source: Text reprinted from Hammond (2014).

> If identity and integrity are more fundamental to good teaching than technique—and if we want to grow as teachers—we must do something alien to academic culture: we must talk to each other about our inner lives—risky stuff in a profession that fears the personal and seeks safety in the technical, the distant, the abstract. (Palmer, 2012)

From Culturally Conscious to Culturally Humble (An Equity Pathway)

In the previous section, it was noted that culture *drives our affirmations for one another and ultimately makes meaning of what happens with us and to us every day.* An established culture represents who we are as an institution, organization, or group (Páez & Albert, 2012). Within these environments, we may or may not be conscious of our interactions and how they are interconnected and, in turn,

FIGURE 1.8   The Cultural Consciousness Matrix

Level 2	Level 3
Consciously Unskilled	Consciously Skilled
• You know that you don't know	• You know that you have the skill
• Beginning of growth	• Comfortable with being uncomfortable
• Crisis of consciousness	• Focused confidence
• Enlightened	• Intentional
Being	**Becoming**
Level 1	Level 4
Unconsciously Unskilled	Unconsciously Skilled
• You don't know what you don't know	• You know the skill and the skill is second nature
• Complete lack of knowledge and skills	• Completely confident
• Fixed mindset	• Automaticity, accountability, humility
• Oblivious	• Graceful
Existing	**Evolving**

Source: Adapted from Burch (1970).

influence our culture. The Cultural Consciousness Matrix (Figure 1.8) is a guide for members of learning communities as they interact and engage with one another and the world around them and evolve from cultural competence to cultural humility. It scaffolds their movement through four levels of knowing.

Level 1: Unconsciously Unskilled The individual does not understand or know the value of recognizing and appreciating dimensions of difference; for example, they are insensitive to oppression, microaggressions, and the systemic disadvantages of others. They have not identified the deficit that restricts their ability to nourish others and themselves. They deny the skill of being **culturally conscious**, which means they don't understand the three levels of culture. The individual must acknowledge their lack of skill and the value of a new skill before moving on to the next level. The duration of time an individual spends at this level depends on the strength of the stimulus to learn.

Level 2: Consciously Unskilled The individual does not understand the skill of being culturally conscious, although they recognize their deficit as well as the value of new skills to address the deficit.

They are cognizant of microinvalidations, microinsults, and their own biases. At Level 2, individuals experience growth and have to function in brave spaces where they take risks, ask questions, share perspectives, and listen to the stories of others. It is uncomfortable because the individual must confront their cultural shortcomings, for example by sharing their own cultural journey, personal background, and racial lenses. The learning community needs to engage in rich and diverse conversations at this level.

Level 3: Consciously Skilled The individual is deliberate in their personal cultural development and utilizes skills to move toward cultural competence by demonstrating a personal cultural expansion and the ability to connect across dimensions of difference. At this level, they are starting the journey of acceptance and, depending upon the context, moving toward appreciation. The movement at this level is contingent upon learning how to manifest behaviors that strive to benefit humankind. This pathway to cultural competence leads to intense consciousness of the realities regarding the systemic maltreatment of others. At Level 3, the individual can recognize the differences between equality and equity and is willing to call out injustice in the world around us. They will experience an emotional charge as they engage in uncomfortable discourse that requires recovery affectively, behaviorally, and cognitively. *"When you can't recover you can't move, and when you can't move you can't breathe."*

Level 4: Unconsciously Skilled The individual has mastered the dimensions of identity and levels of culture and has evolved from cultural competence toward cultural humility. For example, the individual supports the constructs of unconstrained equity, values all aspects of cultural identity, expresses unconditional positive regard, creates spaces of relational trust, and dismantles the "isms" (racism, classism, sexism, ableism, antisemitism, genderism, ageism, nationalism, sizeism, heterosexualism, ethnocentrism, etc.) while displaying a curiosity regarding differences unknown. **Cultural humility** is a process of self-awareness and grace in which we relentlessly challenge the imbalances of power and privilege that impact the way we see ourselves, others, and the world around us as we uphold the principle that human growth is never-ending—it is a journey. At this level you accept that you never really *master* cultural competence. We believe that cultural competence is a paver toward cultural humility—a destination at which we never fully arrive. We must offer ourselves grace and accept guidance for braving the true quest of collective equity.

These levels of knowing position individuals to progressively evolve from being unconscious to conscious, unskilled to skilled, which in turn creates the movement toward collective equity in the learning community and empowers the collective to bridge the knowing-doing gap of cultural consciousness. According to Robbins (2005), cultural proficiency in an organization is reflected in its policies and practices; in an individual, it is the values and behaviors that enable that person to interact effectively in a culturally diverse environment. In a culturally proficient school or organization, the culture promotes inclusiveness and institutionalizes processes for learning about differences and for responding appropriately to differences.

Summary

As we move into the next five chapters of this book, we wish to reinforce the ways in which we engage with each other to ensure there is a consistent focus on decision making and actions required to create brave spaces of learning in schools where systems are transformed so that the learning community:

- comes together as a collective

- fulfills the promise of collective equity

- builds relational trust and motivation

- cultivates cultural humility

Chapter Highlights

- Cultural diversity is consistently increasing in our country and thus in our schools. Since 2014, the majority of students in our public schools have been non-white.

- Our students enter our classrooms with a rich array of identities including race, gender identity, sexual orientation, social class, religion, cognitive ability, physical ability, and family structures.

- When we intentionally understand, honor, and celebrate the dimensions of identity, we can impact teaching, leading, and learning for all.

- There are three levels of culture that impact who we are and how we appear.

- Through our understanding of who we are as educators, who our students are as learners, who the teachers and leaders are as an organization, and who we are as a community, we can engage in consideration of how we close our knowing-doing gap using the Cultural Consciousness Matrix.

Invitation to Collective Thinking

- How will your organization utilize the Collective Equity Framework to foster rich and rigorous conversations and actions to create collective equity?

- How do we capitalize on the personal level of engagement to position ourselves in order to make an impact on the professional and organizational levels? How can we consider the enabling conditions and take action?

- How does knowing yourself culturally impact your relationships and coming together as a collectivist community?

- How can you learn more about your colleagues' deep cultures to cultivate trusting environments and sustain positive working relationships?

Reflection

The Cultural Consciousness Matrix outlines the levels of knowing that empower a collective to bridge the knowing-doing gap.

THE CULTURAL CONSCIOUSNESS MATRIX	
Level 2	Level 3
Consciously Unskilled	Consciously Skilled
• You know that you don't know	• You know that you have the skill
• Beginning of growth	• Comfortable with being uncomfortable
• Crisis of consciousness	• Focused confidence
• Enlightened	• Intentional
Being	**Becoming**

(Continued)

(Continued)

Level 1	Level 4
Unconsciously Unskilled	Unconsciously Skilled
• You don't know what you don't know	• You know the skill and the skill is second nature
• Complete lack of knowledge and skills	• Completely confident
• Fixed mindset	• Automaticity, accountability, humility
• Oblivious	• Graceful
Existing	**Evolving**

Source: Adapted from Burch (1970).

In what ways has the information in Chapter 1 closed your knowing-doing gap?

_____

_____

_____

_____

_____

Who are you culturally as collective?

_____

_____

_____

_____

_____

At what level of the matrix are you, as a collective?

_____

_____

_____

_____

_____

Where do you need to go as a collective to move from being culturally conscious to culturally humble?

_____

_____

_____

_____

_____

Cultivating an Environment of Collective Equity

2

Creating Culture Through Shared Truths, Purpose, Vision, and Mission

There are only two ways to influence human behavior: you can manipulate it or you can inspire it.

—Simon Sinek

As long as our differences (race, sexual orientation, gender, socioeconomic status, family dynamics, immigration status, gender identity, physical ability, religion, ethnicity, cognitive ability, and language) continue to impact how we are seen in the world, we must come together for the common good. More specifically, we must create schools and districts that disrupt policies, structures, and practices that perpetuate marginalizations and systemic inequities. To reiterate, collective equity is a shared responsibility for the social, cultural, academic, and emotional fortification of students and adults that allows for everyone to achieve their goals and aspirations on their own terms. It addresses systemic barriers, historic racism, educational disparities, and levels of oppression by fostering culturally fortifying experiences.

In most school districts and schools, developing a mission statement, vision statement, and statements of belief is a common practice for school leaders. This work resides on websites of districts across the nation, and when you enter any school building you will observe a variety of ways these messages are displayed. However, these statements typically don't include an obligation to disrupt and eliminate persistent disparities together with the practices and policies that negatively impact historically marginalized groups. Moreover, these statements typically don't communicate the actions that must be taken to realize collective equity. Often, these statements are created outside the communities that have committed to "coming together" as defined in Chapter 1. Although many leaders will host sessions to "gain input" from others, they often don't take the necessary steps to provide the learning community with voice, value, and agency in the process of creating shared vision, mission, and beliefs around the achievement of educational equity.

In this chapter, we aim to disrupt the episodic events of creating mission, vision, and belief statements in silos. We define the necessary guideposts that move us along a cohesive pathway toward transformative equitable learning environments. When learning communities synergize around a shared mission, a shared vision, and shared beliefs, there is a shift in the culture that elevates the passion, purpose, and perseverance to dismantle biased behaviors, educational inequities, and marginalized disparities in the collective. Every journey is unique at the personal and professional levels. As we simultaneously evolve and embrace our shared accountability for equity, this journey becomes a focused pathway that gives us direction, guidance, and clarity to fulfill the promise of collective equity while providing coherence across the organization.

From Deficit Thinking to Asset-Based Actions

In order to become a collective, we have to identify and eliminate the deficit ways of thinking and being that hold us prisoner in siloes and perpetuate negative school environments. This requires some heavy lifting, beginning with critically examine our beliefs about how we co-exist with others in our organization. Many world leaders and visionary thinkers have given us the gift of wisdom with respect to how we should treat and relate to one another. Following are three of our favorite examples:

> *We will have to repent in this generation not merely for the hateful words and actions of the bad people, but for the appalling silence of the good people.*
>
> **—Reverend Dr. Martin Luther King, Jr.,**
> ***Letter From the Birmingham Jail*, 1963**

> *Watch your thoughts; they become your words. Watch your words; they become your actions. Watch your actions; they become your habits. Watch your habits; they become your character. Watch your character; it becomes your destiny.*
>
> **—Unknown**

> *Your beliefs become your thoughts.*
>
> **—Mahatma Gandhi**

We know from Hattie and Zierer (2017) that how we think about what we do is more impactful than what we do. This comes to life in *deficit thinking,* which is broadly defined as placing blame on the victim (e.g., "They'll never learn because they come from bad families"). Deficit thinking paralyzes the collective because it feeds the belief that we don't have an impact. It propels us into focusing on the perceived weakness, needs, and problems of individuals and members of society—typically, those who are different from us. Deficit thinking is harmful to ourselves and others. The counternarrative to deficit thinking is to focus on our impact and the strengths of the members in our learning community. Deficit thinking influences our actions as we blame students and families for their cultural representations that are expressed academically, socially, and behaviorally. A catalyst for transformation is to challenge our inner beliefs and thoughts in order to shape our actions. Although no individual action is a revolution, the sum of our daily continuous efforts leads to real transformation (Chugh, 2018).

Shared Truths and Purpose

The collective equity process calls upon the learning community to leverage its resources by actively working to engage all members. We do so by acknowledging and valuing diverse perspectives. The partnerships that we form empower us to develop our vision, mission, and shared truths in the interest of building more equitable environments. Within this process, we shift to creating shared truths that include the identification of beliefs. Too often, merely articulating beliefs isn't enough to reach and sustain our desired state of collective equity. Figure 2.1 offers examples of how common statements of beliefs can become the basis of shared truths.

Shared truths enable us to embrace a common language and fashion a community of trust that engenders authenticity and esteems equity of voice. Our schools are a lot more than a center of student learning. They also represent a self-contained culture, with traditions and expectations that reflect its mission, vision, and beliefs (Gruenert & Whittaker, 2015). By upholding our shared truths, we dedicate our actions to creating transformative equitable cultures.

An urgent sense of purpose is what makes us relentless. It energizes the very core of who we are as individuals and as a collective. Purpose helps us clarify and direct our priorities in order to reach our most important equity goals. Purpose is not a destination; rather, it is a journey that requires ongoing deliberate reflection as we explore what matters most. When we define and own our purpose in schools, our collective motivation is enhanced, allowing us to persevere in spite of challenges

FIGURE 2.1   From Mission, Vision, and Belief Statements to Statements of Shared Truths

From a Common Mission Statement to a Shared Mission Statement

Common Mission Statement:	Shared Mission Statement:
Our mission is to develop well-rounded and thoughtful students prepared to cope with a changing postmodern and globalized world.	Our mission is to cultivate environments of trust in order to develop culturally conscious stewards who embrace change in all dimensions of identity in our globalized community.

From a Common Vision Statement to a Shared Vision Statement

Common Vision Statement:	Shared Vision Statement:
Our vision is a community where all children feel loved, respected, and encouraged to develop to their fullest potential.	Our vision is that we are a learning community where all feel loved, respected, encouraged, and supported to embrace and engage in limitless possibilities.

From Common Statements of Beliefs to Shared Truths Statements

Common Statements of Beliefs:	Shared Truths Statements:
Every student experiences challenging and rigorous learning opportunities.	We believe that in order to provide rigorous and challenging learning opportunities, we must know how to use and remove scaffolds to meet the needs of every learner.
Students and staff respect the individual identities of others.	We believe that the learning community is a place where the individual identities of all members are respected by intentionally greeting each member by name, giving specific and individual feedback, and affirming individual and group contributions.
All students acquire skills to become a lifelong learner in a diverse world.	We believe that fostering learning for a diverse world obliges us to create experiences of world consciousness, identifying historical contributions from all cultures, which will result in meaningful cognitive engagement.
All members of the school community are technologically proficient.	We believe that learning engagements require frequent use of technological tools that amplify the instructional experience for everyone in the learning community.

that create equity fatigue and emotional despair. These challenges are often presented as assessment results, disappointing data, unwilling-ness of others to recognize the need for equity, community push back, lack of skills and knowledge, the belief that equity is "an initiative," initiative fatigue, superficial equity practices, and feelings of failure. Even in a high-performing school, it is still necessary to define and own our purpose in order to strive for inclusion, equity, and excellence for all members of the learning community.

Jot Thought

What differences do you notice between the two types of mission, vision, and belief statements in Figure 2.1?

_____

_____

_____

How do the statements of shared truths create a collective culture?

_____

_____

_____

FIGURE 2.2   Considering the Paths

Image Source: istock.com/francescoch

Vision and Mission Development

We believe the traditional methods of writing organizational mission and vision statements exclusive of shared truths and purpose nullifies the ability to come together and engage as a collective. The counternarrative is co-construction of vision and mission statements that emerge from the shared truths and purpose of the learning community. Moreover, when we engage in collective equity, our vision statements must

1. emphasize inclusivity;

2. illustrate a clear picture of where we are going; and

3. promote a mission that inspires the school community to take collective action and identify the steps toward their destination.

In the field example below, a high school principal encourages his team to identify their shared truths. As you read this example, you will observe that the leader comes to a crossroads where he can choose a traditional path of creating a vision and mission in a virtual silo or leverage his expertise to engage the collective in creating a vision and mission.

> The two most important days in your life are the day you are born and the day you find out why.
>
> —Unknown

Field Example of Creating a Mission and Vision With Shared Truths and Purpose

At Edgewood Academy (EWA), Dr. Flowers leads with a mindframe: "We learn and lead together." This is his 15th year in leadership but his first year at EWA. The demographics at EWA are 85 percent free and reduced lunch, 55 percent Black, 20 percent Hispanic, 20 percent white and 5 percent Asian. The school is static in its academic performance. However, there is a growing opportunity gap between the Black and Hispanic students compared to the white and Asian students. The district administration placed Dr. Flowers at EWA to make an impact on the culture and achievement of historically marginalized students of color.

Over the summer, Dr. Flowers started his school year working with his new leadership team. The work session included discussing EWA's existing mission, vision, and belief statements. He wished to honor their past work as well as better understand where they have been. The team started with sharing the common statements of beliefs. Dr. Flowers inquired about the meaning and intent of current belief statements. As the conversation progressed, it was apparent that the belief statements had no evidence of impact, and some members of the learning community held true to their biased beliefs that inhibited the recognition of who students are and what they can do. One belief that was challenged among the members of the team was "Rigor is for everyone." When this belief was communicated, some members of the team became defensive as they held onto to their biased belief that in order for certain students to experience success, there was a need to lower the expectations and lessen rigor. Misconceptions quickly surfaced, and it became apparent that team members weren't in agreement about which belief statements were shared by all.

At this moment, Dr. Flowers understood the importance of creating shared truths from the existing EWA belief statements. As he listened for understanding, he asked the question, "What does this look like in practice?" The team could not effectively answer the question, and their answers seemed very ambiguous to Dr. Flowers. As he pushed and prodded the team, they were visibly upset and did not know how to (or chose not to) respond to his inquiry. He could see them begin to shut down. Unfortunately, in some schools the vision, mission, and belief statements have little to no impact and feel like mere decorations on the wall. For Dr. Flowers, these reactions were not surprising. At this juncture of the process, Dr. Flowers realized that the team lacked the capacity and the stamina to cognitively or emotionally engage in identifying the meaning of the belief statements and how they look (or don't look) in practice.

In the spirit of perseverance, Dr. Flowers asked the team to individually reflect on each of the belief statements and consider specific actions that might help to actualize the beliefs. The team members shared their individual reflections with each other to identify commonalities and differences in perspectives. This process of sharing created authentic opportunities to build a community of trust in which all voices are honored. The team was now motivated and prepared to reconsider EWA's statements of beliefs and create shared truths to guide their work.

At this stage, leadership teams can adopt the existing vision and mission statements with a few tweaks to the language. However, based upon his experience creating collectives, Dr. Flowers knew that to give the team direction and bring to life their shared truths in daily practices, they needed to include the voices of students and families. Members of the leadership team designed engagement opportunities for each

(Continued)

(Continued)

of the PLCs for the collective purpose of refining the vision and mission statements. This process was replicated with all members of the school community, including the PTA, local business council, and faculty, to ensure consistent communication and commitments to the collective. Dr. Flowers and the team are now prepared to start the year by dedicating their actions to creating a collective equitable culture.

We have observed schools take different pathways to adopting or enhancing their mission, vision, and belief statements. Dr. Flowers' approach enables the learning community to start the school year by taking action to create a transformative, equitable collective culture:

- Engage the leadership team in dialogue about their collective purpose of leading and teaching for all in the learning community, and emphasize the interdependence of shared truths and the vision, mission, and beliefs statements. This process will bring the language to life and gives the team direction and a common destination aligned to their efforts.

- Encourage leadership team members to reveal individual truths in order to empower them to develop shared truths.

- Design engagement opportunities for each of the PLCs to refine the vision, mission, and belief statements to represent the team's shared truths.

- Adopt and communicate with all members of the school community (e.g., PTA, local business council, faculty meetings) to ensure consistent communication and collaborative commitments to the collective.

> Nothing can stop the power of a committed and determined people to make a difference in our society. Why? Because human beings are the most dynamic link to the divine on this planet.
>
> —John Lewis

In the remainder of this book, you will be introduced to five leaders who have cultivated educational spaces that reflect purpose, passion, determination, and educational outcomes that fortify learning communities. These collective equity voices exemplify the interconnection of pedagogy and practice that can realize the promise of transformative equitable environments. Their humanity is both visible and generative in creating systems that focus on all members in their organizations by attending to intentional ways of being a collective.

Shared Experience

Creating Statements of Shared Truths

1. Discuss the language in your current vision, mission, and belief statements and listen for evidence of shared truths.

2. If any statements are void of shared truths and coherence, create shared truths and send them out for the learning community to review and provide feedback, then adopt them with recommended modifications.

3. If there are shared truths in the statements, then adopt them and discuss how the process will be replicated with the greater learning community.

 Available for download from resources.corwin.com/CollectiveEquity

 Collective Equity Voices

Principal Dr. Theresa Yeldell's Journey to Collective Equity

Banner Preparatory School is an alternative high school (Grades 9–12) working in partnership with the Milwaukee Public School District in Wisconsin. It is a small program with a student population that is in constant flux over the course of the school year. The students are assigned by the District as a result of a district hearing for serious disciplinary infractions. This is a temporary assignment ranging from one semester to two years. Over the course of 13 years with the District, Banner Preparatory engaged thousands of students and their families, with the primary goal of helping students to get back on track with their educational and personal journeys.

Banner Prep Mission and Vision: Banner Preparatory High School embraces a philosophy of lifelong learning. We offer a multi-faceted instructional program to address the varied learning needs of our students in order to facilitate their desire to get back on track with their educational journey. We look to provide every opportunity to position our students for success and to instill positivity and hope.

Their focused goals are to work collaboratively to provide quality educational opportunities; engage supportive personnel within a

(Continued)

(Continued)

family-oriented atmosphere; identify and support students' academic and personal strengths; and encourage pathways to graduation and post-secondary/employment options as a result of individual student growth and achievement.

Much of who they are is the result of coming together as a group of educators whose beliefs are rooted in the power of knowing and the desire to offer that power to young people whose journeys have been mired in a combination of missteps, personal and institutional. As they developed their focus and purpose, there was a realization that much of their thinking was in alignment with the Principles of Kwanzaa. This was not intentional but is reflective of the collective experiences of the initial planning by the team.

At the heart of the organization are the principles of collective work and responsibility (Ujima), cooperative economics (Ujamaa), and the importance of collective creative energy (Kuumba). Their belief is that successful teaching and learning is the result of bringing shared truths, purpose, beliefs, and visions together in a way that maximizes the opportunities for growth and progress in the education of the whole child. Banner Prep exemplifies a family perspective. Anyone who enters the Banner Prep world becomes a member of the Banner Prep family. Dr. Yeldell shared that successful staff produces successful students, and successful students strengthen the entire family—"theirs at home and ours at school." Failure is a "not yet" achieved opportunity. It is a time to regroup and find another way to support a student's journey forward. Sometimes that "way" is not with Banner.

The school's mission, vision, and goals are reviewed and discussed annually as a contractual requirement; however, they are at the forefront of discussions and planning throughout the school year. They are posted in every classroom and meeting area of the school, and they are included in parent and community engagement documents. An important practice of Banner Prep is inclusive decision making.

There are 19 staff members (teachers, staff, and administrators). Organizationally, Banner Prep meets as a "team of the whole" that makes decisions by informed consensus. This is important because there are always situations that require "all hands on deck" or immediate intervention by the nearest available adult. There is an understanding of shared responsibility as being essential to daily operations. Any staff member will step in where and when needed. Teams (academic, behavior, and administrative) and subsets of these teams can meet to discuss specific agendas. It is essential to develop practices and procedures that set expectations for the participation of every member of the "family." How did Dr. Yeldell and team get there?

Hiring Procedures. Banner probably has an opportunity that most District schools are not privileged to have. As a contracted school program, they advertise, interview, and hire staff based upon their identified needs. The program components (academic, social, and emotional) guide their decisions, relative to how best to meet the needs of students now and in the future. They chose to include existing staff needs and perspectives in the search for new staff members who will not only fill a curricular need, but will enhance the academic, socio-emotional, and philosophical framework of the school. All staff members are "at-will" hires. There is a mutual understanding that the employee and the school share equal responsibility to determine whether they "fit." The current team is composed of veteran members (who have been with Banner Prep for 6–13 years) and newer members (who have been with Banner Prep for 1–5 years).

Dr. Yeldell and team build relational trust and motivation as a "family." Their mantra is, "Whatever can happen in a family can happen here. Let's deal with it." They learn, plan, communicate, and celebrate together, singing Happy Birthday and eating cake; exercising together with laughter and encouragement; crying and embracing when life has its way. Former staff members, students, and their family members keep in touch to let them know about life successes and sorrows. That is what family means to Banner Prep. That is what brings them to the work and mission.

Realizing collective equity in action:

How did Dr. Yeldell communicate the shared mission, vision, and beliefs to the Banner Preparatory learning community?

How did her passion and focus on inclusionary practices demonstrate collective equity in action?

_____

_____

_____

_____

> How can we really believe that parents and families can come through open doors when the doors of life, equity, opportunities, voice, confidence, security, safety, and justice are never really open to our marginalized communities?
>
> —Nicole and Sonja

Essential Components of Collective Equitable Cultures

In transformative collective equitable cultures, the learning community shares responsibility for implementing the components of collective equity, to provide coherence across the organization. The essential components are listed in Table 2.1.

In a commitment to transformative equitable impact, the learning community leverages fundamental aspects of coherence. Coherence involves a combination of ambitious goals and intentional pathways while being vigilant, committed, and consistent to deepen learning for all (Fullan & Quinn, 2016). In collective equity, the only way to achieve

TABLE 2.1   Essential Components for Creating Collective Equitable Cultures

1. Mindfulness on dimensions of leadership and how we focus, deliver, and assess instruction

2. Community engagement and involvement where school is accessible

3. Programs that support and accelerate all learners

4. Strategic resourcing that addresses inequities

5. Professional development that aligns to the needs of our learning community

6. Expressions of cultural representation that fortify the collective

 Shared Experience

Embedding the Essential Components in Your Learning Community

In the chart below, describe how each of the essential components for creating collective equitable cultures is reflected in your learning community.

ESSENTIAL COMPONENTS	DESCRIPTION	IN YOUR LEARNING COMMUNITY
Mindfulness on dimensions of leadership and how we focus, deliver, and assess instruction	Leaders purposefully call attention to creating an equitable culture, which requires a focus on the following dimensions: pioneering, energizing, affirming, inclusivity, humility, deliberation, and resoluteness (Sugarman, Sullard & Wilhem, 2011). These dimensions are needed to focus, deliver, and assess instruction.	

ESSENTIAL COMPONENTS	DESCRIPTION	IN YOUR LEARNING COMMUNITY
	• Focus: leveraging the actions of the learning community on the shared mission, vision and beliefs	
	• Deliver: strategizing and aligning actions to outcomes	
	• Assess: gathering defined sets of data to conduct an analysis that validates real-time actions of equity	
Programs that support and accelerate all learners	Programs provide solutions to equity stumbling blocks that hinder transformation of the learning community. Such programs are intended to support and accelerate all learners:	
	• Support: designing opportunities for the members of the learning community to respond to identified needs with immediacy	
	• Accelerate: cultivating an environment to reduce inequities with an intense focus and velocity	
Strategic resourcing that addresses inequities	The learning community proactively makes decisions regarding resources (people, programs, and professional development) that specifically addresses inequities.	
	• Addressing inequities: mobilizing the supports for organizational learning by eradicating barriers that oppress the movement of the collective	
Professional development that aligns to the needs of our learning community	Professional development improves knowledge, attitudes, and skills for systemic transformation.	
	• Aligns to the needs of the learning community: adjusting actions as a result of intentional scrutiny of organizational disparities that impede learning for all	
Expressions of cultural representations that fortify the collective	Culturally fortifying experiences are integral to being a collective.	
	• Cultural representations: Producing and exchanging meaning between members of a culture through the use of language, unspoken rules, unconscious beliefs and norms, and hidden dynamics	
	• Fortify the collective: Strengthening and enhancing the individual and the collective by prioritizing the good of the society over the welfare of the individual	

(Continued)

(Continued)

ESSENTIAL COMPONENTS	DESCRIPTION	IN YOUR LEARNING COMMUNITY
Community engagement and involvement where school is accessible	All members of the learning community contribute, invest in, and learn from each other. • School is accessible: providing approaches to reach intended outcomes that are designed to benefit all members of the community	

 Available for download from resources.corwin.com/CollectiveEquity

coherence is by providing opportunities for engagement that require a shared depth of understanding of our purpose, monitoring the implementation of our essential components, and being collectively accountable for our results. The only way to achieve coherence in a collective culture is through the interdependence of its essential components, depicted in Figure 2.3.

Collective Engagement by Design Process

Designing the scope of the work calls upon the collective to have clarity on their purpose; deeply immerse themselves in a cycle of analysis of the essential components; and examine the results that align to the shifts in approaches, actions, and attitudes. When the learning community comes together around this process, they embrace the primary function of collective equity. We call this the collective engagement by design process. Incorporating this three-stage model is the catalyst for organizational transformation and strengthening the collective. Figure 2.4 depicts the design process of implementing, monitoring, and assessing. The purpose of the collective undergirds the essential components and results that show the impact of deep and sustained equitable practices, processes, and structures for the learning community.

Purpose, which is depicted as the foundation of the pyramid, is the driving force that motivates us and reinforces our collective commitment to remove barriers that impede the process. Without a clear purpose this process is null and void. We have observed too many teams that

FIGURE 2.3   Interdependent Essential Components for Creating Collective Equitable Cultures

FIGURE 2.4   Collective Engagement by Design Process

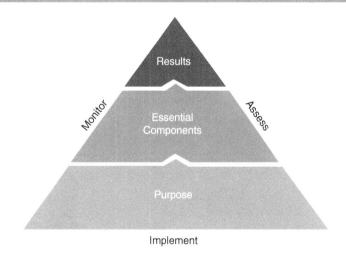

don't know where they are going, how they will get there, and when they have arrived. This creates divisiveness because there is no equity vision, which results in stagnation that deflates the spirit of a shared mission and well-intended equity goals. The collective engagement by design process gives strength and brings breath to the learning community. When the community is united, we can better analyze each essential component with a shared purpose.

By focusing on the essential components, we can define the course of action to build and sustain collective equitable cultures. Too often the work of creating equity cultures is weakened because there is little to no monitoring and assessing the implementation of the collective's actions. In addition, teams do not dig deep to uncover patterns of inequity; they skim the results when reviewing data without acknowledging who is showing up or not (or whose voice is being heard). Safir and Dugan, in their book *Street Data* (2021), take an equitable stance in the development of an actionable framework for school transformation. Their focus disrupts "fixing" and "filling" academic gaps in order to rebuild the system from the *student* up. *Street Data* reminds us of the importance of including students' brilliance, cultural wealth, and intellectual potential when valuing data that is humanizing, liberating, and healing. In other words, learning communities need to acknowledge their current realities when analyzing data, including who is benefitting and who is not (Fisher et al., 2019). Our moral imperative motivates us to determine the impact of our work on addressing educational inequities and marginalizations.

Summary

When we come together to create our shared truths and give credence to our purpose, we are then positioned to proclaim a mission and vision that synergizes the work. As we identified in Chapter 1, collective equity is a process in which the learning community works together, sharing accountability and thus shaping a transformative equitable learning environment. In this chapter, statements of shared truths and a shared purpose are the pillars to a unified vision and mission. This instrumental step empowers us to design coherence and depth of understanding around the nature of our work, creating learning cultures that fulfill the promise of collective equity.

Chapter Highlights

- In most school districts and schools, there is an expectation that school leaders will create vision, mission, and beliefs statements.

- Too often, vision, mission, and belief statements are created without the input of the community that is committed to coming together as defined in Chapter 1.

- In the collective equity process, the learning community leverages its resources by activity working to engage all members. This allows the collective to acknowledge and value diverse perspectives, thus creating a partnership that enhances and empowers the development of a vision, mission, and shared truths.

- Shared truths enable us to embrace a common language, fashioning a community of trust that illustrates authenticity and esteems equity of voice.

- Purpose is what makes us relentless. It energizes the very core of who we are as individuals and as a collective. Purpose gives us direction and helps us to clarify our priorities, creating a tenacity to accomplish what we aim to achieve.

- We believe the traditional method of writing organizational mission and vision statements exclusive of shared truths and purpose nullifies the ability to come together and engage as a collective.

- In equitable school cultures, the learning community shares responsibility to provide coherence across the entire organization.

- The essential components of collective equity build our competence around our purpose; actions, skills, and attitudes frame and reinforce our internal and external shared accountability to the collective, thus resulting in deep equitable impact on the organization.

- When we come together and create our shared truths and purpose, we are then positioned to give life to a mission and vision that can fulfill the promise of collective equity.

Invitation to Collective Thinking

- How will you pay attention to voice, value, and agency in the systems and structures of your learning community?

- How does your learning community leverage resources by actively working to engage all members of the collective?

- What are the shared truths, purpose, vision, and mission of your learning community?

- Using the collective engagement by design process, identify examples of how you can leverage your learning community's purpose and the essential components to achieve collective equity.

Reflection

The Cultural Consciousness Matrix below outlines the levels of knowing that empower a collective to bridge the knowing-doing gap.

THE CULTURAL CONSCIOUSNESS MATRIX	
Level 2	Level 3
Consciously Unskilled	Consciously Skilled
• You know that you don't know	• You know that you have the skill
• Beginning of growth	• Comfortable with being uncomfortable
• Crisis of consciousness	• Focused confidence
• Enlightened	• Intentional
Being	**Becoming**
Level 1	Level 4
Unconsciously Unskilled	Unconsciously Skilled
• You don't know what you don't know	• You know the skill and the skill is second nature
• Complete lack of knowledge and skills	• Completely confident
• Fixed mindset	• Automaticity, accountability, humility
• Oblivious	• Graceful
Existing	**Evolving**

Source: Adapted from Burch (1970).

In what ways has the information in Chapter 2 closed your knowing-doing gap?

_____

_____

_____

_____

What is your knowing-doing gap?

_____

_____

_____

_____

So what does this mean to you?

_____

_____

_____

_____

Now what are your immediate actions?

_____

_____

_____

_____

Enacting Motivation and Relational Trust for the Collective Equity Movement

3

The Glue That Bonds Us Together

///

We can disagree and still love each other. Unless your disagreement is rooted in my oppression and denial of my humanity and right to exist.

—James Baldwin

What motivates individuals to form and engage in movements? Movements require action, inspiration, strength, perseverance, courage, commitment, and focus. To create a movement we must acknowledge the role that human emotions, behaviors and dispositions play in why some movements succeed and others fail. The power to impact a movement lies within collective actions. Actions are accelerated when individuals come together for a common purpose in the achievement of the common goal. The motivation towards the common goal is the glue that bonds the collective together and sustains the movement. As well, a person can be motivated to act within a movement for reasons beyond their personal and collective identities. Examples include white Americans who participate in the Black Lives Matter movement, men who attend women's marches, and heterosexuals who participate in Pride celebrations (Radke, Kutlaca, Siem, Wright, & Becker, 2020),

Human motivation has long been a subject of interest, from Abraham Maslow's *A Theory of Human Motivation* (1943) to more current publications such as Daniel Pink's *Drive: The Surprising Truth About What Motivates Us* (2009). Maslow's motivation hierarchy is typically depicted as a pyramid. At the bottom of the pyramid are extrinsic (physiological) needs such as food and shelter. As we progress up the pyramid, the focus shifts to intrinsic needs such as the need for esteem and self-actualization. Pink's framework, discussed later in this chapter, primarily focuses on intrinsic motivators. What they have in common is an emphasis on personal or individual factors that motivate humans. In a collectivist culture, humans are motivated by the needs and goals of the group rather than the needs and desires of each individual. In such cultures, relationships and the interconnectedness of people are central to each person's identity and motivation.

We can't aspire to be our personal best without also aspiring to treat our fellow learning community members in a balanced and supportive way. When the collective comes together and we begin to build relationships with one another, we are empowered to co-construct our shared purpose and maintain a focus on the work. However, in the absence of trust, maintaining such a focus is unlikely. Non-trust is a barrier to motivation and a contributor to unproductive environments where there is no progress, no communication, and no connectivity.

Competence, reliability, integrity, and communication are a few traits often associated with creating trust in collective environments. Where there's trust, researchers say, people are more likely to innovate because they feel less vulnerable and alone (von Frank, 2010). "Trust is an individual's or group's willingness to be vulnerable to another party based on the confidence that the latter party is benevolent, reliable, competent, honest, humble, and open" (Tschannen-Moran, 2003). Trust is essential if an organization is to succeed.

Building trust in organizations is ongoing and requires attention to the actions taken by the group. Also, trust alone does not guarantee the interconnectedness of members of the collective. "You can ignore the principles that govern trust—but they will not ignore you" (Covey, 2008).

Shared Experience

Barriers to Motivation and Trust

In order for learning communities to progress on the pathway to collective equity, barriers have to be removed so that motivation and trust among the members of the learning community can exist.

WHAT BARRIERS EXIST THAT INHIBIT MOTIVATION AND TRUST IN YOUR LEARNING COMMUNITY?	WHAT CONDITIONS MUST GIVE WAY FOR MOTIVATION AND TRUST TO EXIST IN YOUR LEARNING COMMUNITY?

 Available for download from resources.corwin.com/CollectiveEquity

Relational Trust

The quote above from Steven Covey underscores the power of trust in building and sustaining healthy organizations. In our context, trust accelerates the learning, the purpose, and the focus of our work as a collective. Researchers on trust identify a symbiotic relationship between trust and the mutual interdependence of the members of a group (Bryk & Schneider, 2002; Tschannen-Moran & Gareis, 2015). Bryk and Schneider (2002) describe relational trust as a social phenomenon that is manifested by shared perceptions and beliefs in the school community. As they do when drafting shared truths or mission, vision, and belief statements, the learning community must reach an accord to create relational trust.

Relational trust emerges from authentic interactions in the relational networks of a school (teacher-parent, principal-teacher, teacher-teacher, teacher-student, student-student, school-community). In Bryk and Schneider's 2002 research, relational trust was a resource for school improvement. In schools characterized by high relational trust, educators were more likely to experiment with new practices and work together with parents to advance improvements. As a result, students were more likely to demonstrate marked gains in learning.

For example, in many districts, the adoption of new standards evokes uncertainty and controversy, especially when it is executed in a vacuum. However, we have observed that when all members of the learning community are offered an opportunity to engage before new standards are adopted, relational trust increases. Protocols must be in place to provide members of the collective with the time, space, and equity of voice to discuss the implementation of the standards and how they align to the shared mission, vision, and beliefs of the organization. This

✎ Jot Thought

Considering the symbiotic roles of the members of your learning community, how do you discern each other's intentions, beliefs, and actions? How do these lead to equitable school improvements? Provide some examples.

_____

_____

_____

_____

_____

_____

_____

_____

provides validation of concerns, clarification of the purpose, and the identification process to effectively execute the standards. When we model inclusivity and engage all voices around, we demonstrate transparency, integrity, and, ultimately, build relational trust.

Figure 3.1 is a conceptual framework of relational trust between teachers and principals in a school community (Bryk & Schneider, 2002; Tschannen-Moran & Gareis, 2015). Most notably, the framework includes the five key facets of relational trust identified by Hoy and Tschannen-Moran (1999): benevolence, reliability, competence, honesty, and openness.

FIGURE 3.1   Conceptual Framework of Relational Trust

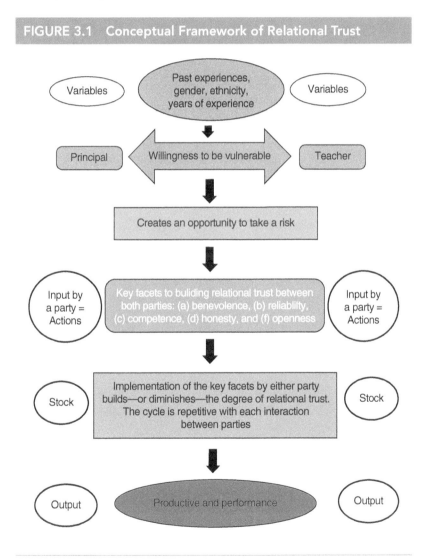

Source: Tennenbaum, Shawn, "Relational Trust within an Urban Public Comprehensive High School District in Northern California" (2018). *Dissertations.* 21.

DOI: https://doi.org/10.31979/etd.6qhg-8xa2

https://scholarworks.sjsu.edu/etd_dissertations/21

Note that Figure 3.1 represents the systemic nature of building relational trust in a hierarchical relationship between a teacher and a principal. However, in our collective, relational trust is based upon role interdependence (principal, teacher, student, parent, and community). Bryk and Schneider (2002) describe relational trust as a social phenomenon that is manifested by the shared perceptions and beliefs of the role groups in the school community. In contrast, we've emphasized the need for the collective to co-create those shared truths, mission, vision, and beliefs.

There are many variables (dimensions of difference), such as past experiences, race/ethnicity, gender, and years of experience, that contribute to how one party views another party prior to allowing oneself to become vulnerable and create relational trust. In the absence of prior contact with a person or institution," Bryk and Schneider (2003), "participants may rely on the general reputation of the other and also on commonalities of race, gender, age, religion, or upbringing" to assess how trustworthy they are (pp. 41–42). This reflects the importance of knowing the levels of culture. When we pick and choose only those aspects of culture that we are comfortable embracing, we choose to not see people who embrace other ways of knowing. We also choose to decrease the opportunity for us to connect beyond a surface level, thereby impacting the way we work together and support a healthy, thriving learning community. According to Hammond (2015), cultural awareness builds rapport and trust between people.

The more interaction members of the learning community have over time, the more willing they are to become vulnerable with one another and build relational trust. "Without one party willing to become vulnerable to another party, the system of building relational trust does not occur" (Bryk & Schneider, 2002). Understanding dimensions of difference allows us to be culturally aware and examine our own identity. This understanding influences and intersects with our personal, relational, professional, organizational, and systemic levels of consciousness in the environment around us—our Collective Equity Framework. When we embrace who we are and we are able to see the value that we add to the wholeness of the community, we can create group harmony as a collective. The dynamic nature of creating relational trust is a cyclical relationship of inputs and outputs with a codependent nexus of shared beliefs, intentions, and actions. The members of the collective are then positioned to develop mutual interdependence and build equitable learning environments in a circle of trust.

The Circle of Trust Approach

"The circle of trust approach is distinguished by principles and practices intended to create a process of shared exploration where people can find a safe space to nurture personal and professional integrity and the courage to act on it." (Palmer, 2004). The organization takes an inner journey that requires a willingness to embrace becoming a collective. By cultivating trust and the reciprocity of trustworthiness, the collective can support and sustain the journey toward undivided beliefs, intentions, and actions.

As educators, Nicole and Sonja have walked the hallways of schools, sat in the seats of many classrooms, and led numerous parent-teacher and community engagements, observing layers of systemic issues that perpetuated inequities for Black and Latinx students. We have seen English learners sitting on the periphery in the back of classrooms with headsets on *as big as their heads* for the entire school day, with little to no interaction with the teacher or their peers; in Black urban schools, outdated textbooks with no mirror opportunities for students to see themselves and their cultural representations; media centers with books that are falling apart; and parents without equity in voice because they trusted in the moral imperative of educating every student to the highest level. There are many questions that we continue to ask: Who is engaged and who is not? Whose voice is heard and whose voice is not? Who are the authors in our classroom libraries? Who is being yelled at in the hallways? Who is in the principal's office sitting with their heads down? Who is being blamed and who is being shamed? Whose affective filter is being increased? Who does not say one word in all of their classrooms? Who sits by the teacher and who is in the back of the class? Who gets feedback and who gets ignored? Who gets the smiles and who gets the still face? What is the professional development that teachers are receiving and who is leading it? Which parents are participating in the PTO? Who is being remediated and who is being accelerated? Who is failing and who is not? Who is being retained? Who is reading on grade level and who is not? Who gets the worksheets and who gets the performance-based projects? Who is being suspended and who just gets detention? Who smiles and who does not? Who is graduating and who is not? *Who is just surviving and who is thriving?*

Until we are willing to answer the questions above and recognize the inequities within the answers, *we will never fulfill the promise of collective equity.* If we are compelled to become a collective and not do this work alone, value will be placed on creating trustworthy relationships that sustain us as we embark on the journey of real equity transformation. It will require becoming a tenacious community of support, motivation, and courage to form a "circle of trust."

The Art of the Heart

Sometimes the heart sees what is invisible to the eye.

—H. Jackson Brown

The social unrest and protest movement in response to acts of police brutality against African Americans in 2020 and 2021 was a vivid call to action that cut across dimensions of identities around the world. We shared potent emotions of the human heart when we all observed George Floyd call for his "mama" as he took his last breath. These emotions ran the gamut from sadness, despair, depression, anger, hatred, disgust, disdain, fear, disbelief, sorrow, fury, bitterness, perplexity, desperation, to outrage. An awakening spread across co-conspirators, allies, advocates, abolitionists, accomplices, and anti-racists who wailed, mourned, and lamented for justice as we gripped our hearts. This was a humanistic conviction of the heart that required us to act. It thrust the collective into movement and we experienced the possibilities of coming together. Once we came together, we knew that we needed to be together threaded by our unconscious connection and interdependence of being human—the Art of the Heart.

Relational trust is built on movements of the human heart such as empathy, commitment, compassion, patience, and the capacity to forgive.

—Parker J. Palmer

Often we discuss the Golden Rule, which is to treat people the way we want to be treated. A counternarrative to the Golden Rule is the *Platinum Rule,* which reminds us to treat others the way *they* want and need to be treated. This mindset is allocentric in that it puts the focus on others and is tailored to a collectivist approach rather than an individualistic way of being. As Palmer (2012) noted, there are movements of the human heart that build relational trust in organizations. We call these movements the stimuli of building relational trust (see Figure 3.2).

Organizations need these stimuli to propel them forward to focus on matters of the heart. The stimuli of building relational trust exist to rouse high levels of energy to transform the learning community for the benefit of all. This is not something that occurs as a single episodic event; rather, it is enacted over time.

FIGURE 3.2   The Stimuli of Building Relational Trust
Empathy
Commitment
Compassion
Patience
Capacity to Forgive

Jot Thought

Define these terms in your own words, focusing on what they look like, sound like, and feel like in your learning community.

THE STIMULI OF BUILDING RELATIONAL TRUST

Empathy

- Looks like: _____

- Sounds like: _____

- Feels like: _____

Commitment

- Looks like: _____

- Sounds like: _____

- Feels like: _____

Compassion

- Looks like: _____

- Sounds like: _____

- Feels like: _____

Patience

- Looks like: _____

- Sounds like: _____

- Feels like: _____

The Capacity to Forgive

- Looks like: _____

- Sounds like: _____

- Feels like: _____

 Available for download from resources.corwin.com/CollectiveEquity

The Stimuli of Building Relational Trust

Empathy

Empathy is the internal capacity to understand, recognize, and share the thoughts and feelings of others. It is critical when establishing and sustaining relationships. Because of our common purpose and a desire to share obligations while maintaining expectations, we must be open to varying perspectives and view others through the lens of empathy. When we can see a challenge, barrier, or stumbling block through the eyes of others, we validate their lived experience. Empathy builds a positive organizational culture that flourishes when there is relational trust among the collective.

Commitment

Commitment, in the context of our work, is one's level of enthusiasm for personal, relational, professional, organizational, and systemic transformation. It is a feeling of responsibility regarding the shared truths, mission, vision, and beliefs of the organization. This level of responsibility doesn't happen overnight. But when we can validate and celebrate our vulnerabilities and the ability to unlearn, update, refine, and reconsider our knowledge, attitudes, and skills, our commitment to the collective is accelerated. Commitment is the birthplace of stamina, and where there is stamina there is focus and shared accountability, and where there is shared accountability to a shared purpose there is inherent acceleration of the collective.

Compassion

Compassion is the consciousness of the heart when we recognize distress, suffering, and oppression in others. It starts with empathy, the ability to understand others' pain. Compassion goes a step further to soothe life's harshness. It embodies authentic and kind expressions that cultivate harmony within the learning community. Compassion requires us to understand others' perspectives and ways of being. When there is a willingness to understand others' lived experiences, our capacity for expressing compassion is strengthened. Our human compassion binds us to one another not in pity, but as human beings (Mandela, 2012). Compassion motivates us to intentionally demonstrate loving kindness to ourselves and others; it lifts us from stagnation and acceptance of the systems of oppression that are so deeply entrenched in our institutions.

🗨️ Collective Equity Voices
Dr. Denita Harris's Journey to Collective Equity

Dr. Denita Harris started leading the equity journey for the MSD of Wayne Township in 2011, when she became a curriculum coordinator of equity for the district. There had always been other administrators in this role, so leadership in this area was not new, but now it was going to be different.

The equity work had always involved district and school leadership, along with key personnel from schools who wanted to be involved. Individuals could opt in or out, depending on their equity interests and experiences. As Denita entered her new role, she picked up where her predecessor had left off in the area of professional development.

Professional development had been the main area of focus for the district equity team along with designing the new teacher onboarding course, at the time titled, "Environmental Profile." This particular course, along with several others, was required of all new teachers in their first two years of employment, to engage them in learning more about diversity in the district. District equity team meetings occurred throughout the year and were facilitated by an outside consultant who focused on sharing the disproportionality of standardized testing data, as well as having participants engage in identity work. They had an equity plan, but that was all it was, a plan with no direction for execution. As the years passed, the demand and the need to see equitable results increased.

In the fall of 2015, the team shifted from meeting after school and having approximately 40 members to meeting full day with 90 members, including the superintendent, Dr. Jeff Butts. As an equity leader, Dr. Harris understood that changing the system began with working on its people. This began with the realization that the educational institution in which they worked did not design itself; it was designed by people with certain preconceived notions of certain groups of students. If they were really going to change the system and create a plan that was going to benefit the students, staff, and community, they had to get to the root of the system. Although schools were required to have site

(Continued)

(Continued)

representation, many building administrators did not participate and chose to send only one representative. Dr. Harris asked sites to set goals by utilizing the district equity plan and to come back to report what they were doing at their respective sites. But without adequate participation of building leadership, it was still hard to see true change in people that could result in a true change of the system.

In the 2019–2020 school year, the district equity leadership team was born. This leadership group consists of 14 members with representation from the following areas: Superintendent's Cabinet, district administrators, building administrators, guidance, Office of Special Services, teachers, and parent liaisons. This team was given the task of building capacity from within by facilitating both book study groups and racial affinity groups for 240 members. The district started with three books: *So You Want to Talk about Race* by Ijeoma Oluo, *White Fragility* by Robin Diangelo, and *Biased* by Jennifer Eberhardt. Each book study had two diverse facilitators who led discussions on the book, including addressing racism and the implications for their work as educators. There was intense dialogue about identities, life experiences, and how racism plays out in the schools. After the two half-day sessions, district equity team members joined their racial affinity group, led by other members of the leadership team.

The leadership team started sharing monthly lessons for school sites and departments in the spring of 2020. Each equity team meeting was led by building administrators or district department administrators. It remains extremely important for the district to have leaders who understand racial equity and the impact of oppression on students, staff, and families who are Black, indigenous, and people of color. Although the pandemic and social unrest of 2020 was grievous and disheartening, it reinforced the need to address racial inequities in society and within the school systems.

The MSD of Wayne Township board of education adopted an anti-racist resolution in the summer of 2020, which strengthened their work and sent a strong message to the community that there was no room in the district to be non-racist; instead, they were moving forward to becoming an anti-racist institution.

Even during the pandemic, the district equity leadership team decided their equity journey would continue in a virtual space. They started the school year by rotating books and having these discussions during one-hour district equity team meetings. Racial affinity groups also followed this format. As they prepared for the second semester, shared monthly lessons for school sites and departments were provided for the remainder of the year. In addition to the professional learning and racial affinity groups, the district launched an equity website and YouTube channel where they host virtual staff and community circles. They have not arrived at the end of their journey and are not sure if they ever will, but they are proud to say they have been able to move the needle in the right direction and will continue to press forward towards equity.

Realizing collective equity in action:

Identify Dr. Harris's personal, relational, professional, and organizational actions for systemic transformation.

How did her commitment to Wayne Township's equity journey demonstrate collective equity in action?

_____

_____

_____

_____

Patience

Patience is a virtue that demands self-awareness, emotional intelligence, and relational trust. It enables us to persevere through the professional and personal hardships of life. It is the ability to overcome unavoidable obstacles as we remain determined and focused to achieve our collective goals. When we enter empathic and equitable spaces, we are more likely to remain patient when there is relational trust. According to Newman (2016), patient people tend to be more cooperative, more empathic, more equitable, and more forgiving. "Patience involves emphatically assuming some personal discomfort to alleviate the suffering of those around us" (Comer & Sekerka, 2014). When relating to others in the organization, patience becomes a form of kindness. Think of a time when a coworker constantly asked you to share new ideas and how you were willing to share them each time—no matter how many times they asked you. Patience is not founded on reciprocity; rather, it is about one's generosity and compassion. Patience also supports goal attainment. As we patiently experience the inevitable stumbling blocks and disappointments, we remain clear in our conviction that we have the collective capacity to transform our learning environments to more equitable spaces.

Capacity to Forgive

Our capacity to forgive is human nature. Forgiveness enables us to sustain and enhance our relationships. Genuine forgiveness is central not only to individual development but to the development of the collective. It involves the elimination of negative feelings toward others and even ourselves. It feeds relational trust and gives us the ability to constructively respond to feelings of hurt and humiliation. "One moment of anger can wipe out a lifetime of merit" (Dalai Lama). The cultivation of empathy, commitment, compassion, and patience grants us the capacity to forgive. The stimulus of forgiveness is aroused by the energy that drives the beating of the heart. It is that muscle that gives the organization life. Once you stop forgiving, you stop living.

👥 Shared Experience

Describe the ways each of the stimuli can be used to build relational trust in your learning community.

STIMULI OF BUILDING RELATIONAL TRUST	EVIDENCE IN ACTION	EVIDENCE IN INACTION	POSSIBLE PATHWAYS AND PAVERS IN YOUR ORGANIZATION
Empathy			
Commitment			
Compassion			
Patience			
Forgiveness			

Motivation to Nurture the Collective

Earlier in the chapter we touched upon motivation, particularly the distinction between intrinsic and extrinsic rewards. Extrinsic rewards include our paychecks, our cars, and such luxuries as fine jewelry or apparel. For our students, an extrinsic reward might be the promise of a good grade. Intrinsic rewards include the sense of personal gratification that can come from helping others, promoting fairness and justice, or simply meeting a "personal best" goal that we set for ourselves. Rewards and punishments are extrinsic motivators. Most of us have learned from personal experience that while such "carrots and sticks" may impact our behaviors in the short term, they don't improve performance in a deep way or create long-lasting change. The intrinsic motivation of the collective is the desire to achieve our shared mission, vision, beliefs, and purpose.

> We cannot afford to wallow in our discomfort regarding issues of race and equity.
>
> —Dena Simmons

When the collective is vested in doing the work, we see the glass as half full and we are intrinsically motivated. We collectively summon the social, emotional, behavioral, and cognitive forces that get the results we desire—sometimes even taking risks in the process. We are spurred into action without provocation other than our own sense of moral imperative, which draws from the human tendency to seek and overcome challenges and engage in personal growth and development.

According to Pink (2009), motivation has three components:

- Activation

- Persistence

- Intensity

Figure 3.3 defines each of these components. Figure 3.4 illustrates the motivational process as it relates to nurturing the collective.

FIGURE 3.3   Components of Motivation

ACTIVATION	The decision to initiate a behavior in order to achieve the goal
PERSISTENCE	The continued effort to achieve the goal
INTENSITY	The focus, energy, and attention needed to achieve the goal

FIGURE 3.4   Motivation to Nurture the Collective

COMPONENTS OF MOTIVATION	DEFINITIONS	STEPS TO NURTURE THE COLLECTIVE
Activation	The decision to initiate a behavior in order to achieve the goal	• Define the shared mission, vision, and purpose. • Start building relational trust across the learning community. • Identify pathways and pavers for creating collective equity.
Persistence	The continued effort to achieve the goal	• Monitor and assess the implementation of equitable practices, processes, structures, and systems. • Leverage the collective within the learning community. • Celebrate the movement toward equitable transformative learning communities.
Intensity	The focus, energy, and attention needed to achieve the goal	• Implement the enabling conditions (see Chapter 1) as a continuous reflective process that is the north star to the work of collective equity. • Monitor progress in creating transformative equitable learning environments (pathways and pavers). • Use the Cultural Consciousness Matrix (see Chapter 1) to guide the collective in all areas of the Collective Equity Framework.

 Shared Experience

How does your learning community use the components of motivation to nurture the collective and measure impact?

COMPONENTS OF MOTIVATION	DEFINITIONS	STEPS TO NURTURE THE COLLECTIVE
Activation	The decision to initiate a behavior in order to achieve the goal	
Persistence	The continued effort to achieve the goal	
Intensity	The focus, energy, and attention needed to achieve the goal	

 Available for download from resources.corwin.com/CollectiveEquity

Can We Breathe?

In collective learning communities, there is reciprocity; the members share the accountability for nurturing one another. There is no way you can take my breath away if you see me, hear me, feel me, and embrace the humility to nurture me as a human. Howard (2016) has used the terms *head, hands,* and *heart* to understand the interplay of the facets of being human. Knowing this, we must engage all three facets as we nurture others. Motivation is then rooted in a visceral experience in which the heart, the head, and the hands work together to move us from feeling to thinking and from thinking to acting on behalf of the collective. This interdependence serves as a multiplier that generates the conditions to create transformative equitable learning environments. When the environment nurtures who we are individually, relationally, and professionally, we are stimulated, inspired, and motivated to intentionally interrupt structures that breed isolation—a catalyst to the inequities reinforcing systemic oppression. Figure 3.5 lists examples of structures in schools that breed isolation and perpetuate systemic oppression and the alternatives to those structures.

FIGURE 3.5 Structures That Breed Isolation vs. Alternatives to Those Structures

STRUCTURES THAT BREED ISOLATION AND OPPRESSION	ALTERNATIVES TO ISOLATION AND OPPRESSION
Remediation	Acceleration
Experienced teachers	Expert teachers
Zero-tolerance disciplinary practices	Restorative practices
Diversity	Anti-racism

Immersive Experience

Read the narrative below and engage in the **Jot Thought** to tap into your inner experience using the examples in Figure 3.5 of structures that breed isolation.

Diverse Friends Day by Paul C. Gorski and Seema Pothini

When Mr. Carbondale started teaching at Lozen School more than 20 years ago, the students, like the teachers and administrators, were all white.

This began to change 10 years ago when gentrification started driving more families of color out of the city to seek affordable housing. Now more than 40 percent of the student body was composed of students of color. Mr. Carbondale was happy to see the racial demographics of the student body changing.

Mr. Carbondale often volunteered to represent his school at the day-long "Inclusion Excellence" conference hosted each year by his district. At the most recent of these conferences, he found one idea most intriguing: Diverse Friends Day. Students were encouraged to spend one day interacting with classmates with whom they normally wouldn't interact. They would eat lunch at a new table, sit with different people during class, and challenge themselves to shake up their social groups in other ways. The goal was to encourage greater intergroup interaction, especially across race.

Mr. Carbondale told students about Diverse Friends Day; a few protested, while others seemed excited. He noted, though, that Pam and Tariq, the two African American students in his class, and Julio, one of the three Mexican American students in his class, remained silent. Not wanting to put them on the spot, he decided to reach out to them after class. Once class ended, Mr. Carbondale pulled them aside and asked their thoughts on Diverse Friends Day.

"They mean well, but this activity is racist," Pam shared.

"I don't know about racist," Tariq responded, "but I don't want to do it."

Julio added, "I think it sounds kinda fun, but a lot of the white students don't like us and call us names. I don't want to be forced to hang out with white people who do that."

Mr. Carbondale asked Pam to elaborate on her observation that Diverse Friends Day is racist. "There's a lot of racism in this school," she insisted. She wondered how disturbing her lunch—the only time she could relax in a predominantly white school—was going to change that. "I think Diverse Friends Day is for white people," she concluded.

✎ Jot Thought

Tap into your inner experience

What was your Diverse Friends Day?

_____

_____

_____

What factors in this narrative breed isolation?

_____

_____

_____

Which of the examples of structures in Figure 3.5 relate the most to this narrative?

_____

_____

_____

How are inequities cultivated in this scenario for the students, teachers, and organization?

_____

_____

_____

What are the stumbling blocks that impede Mr. Carbondale from meeting his goal?

_____

_____

_____

Shared Experience

- Discuss your responses to the Jot Thought with two to three equity partners.

- Identify areas of varying perspective.

- What pathways and pavers can be considered to strengthen inclusion and community within this scenario? Record four or five ideas on sticky notes (one idea per note).

- Generate an Affinity Map. (See instructions below.)

- Incorporate the ideas and themes from the Affinity Map into a shared school goal to strengthen inclusion and community within the collective.

Affinity Map

1. After recording each idea on a separate sticky note, attach all the sticky notes to a wall, in no particular order.

2. Sort the notes by grouping similar or related ideas together.

3. Discuss with your equity partners what makes the ideas in each group similar, identifying the general topic or category that all items in the group share. Make changes and move sticky notes around as necessary. When the ideas are grouped to your satisfaction, write each group's topic or category name on a card and stick it to the wall above the group.

Intent Versus Impact

We often hear educators say that they have instituted structures with the *intent* to address the inequities in their learning communities. They become very frustrated when their efforts don't have the impact they hoped. Unfortunately, we see them lose their motivation to keep the fight going. Recall Mr. Carbondale's narrative: He exhibited a genuine *intent* to bring diversity and inclusion to the student body, but the *impact* of scheduling contrived interactions had the reverse effect on the students of color. His student Pam shared that Diverse Friends Day was racist and infringed upon her time with her social group.

Was Pam wrong to think Diverse Friends Day is for white people? Gorski and Pothini (2018) provided insight into Pam's reaction:

> *Is she wrong? I don't think so, especially in the absence of more serious racial equity efforts, which these students agreed were missing from their school. Many schools' "celebrating diversity" initiatives are crafted to help white students learn about diversity—not racism, but diversity—in ways that will be most comfortable for them. In some cases, students of color are used essentially as props for the gentle diversity education of white students through activities like Diverse Friends Day. This allows white people to opt out of considering racial justice while deriving social and cultural benefits from diversity awareness. It creates the illusion of diversity appreciation while entrenching inequity. Requiring students of color to participate in these diversity spectacles while failing to attend adequately to inequity can be exploitive. Pam, Tariq, and Julio didn't need to share lunch with white students to learn about difference, much less how racism operated around them. They developed these insights as a matter of survival. White educators were asking them to celebrate a diversity in which their experiences were invisible. This is one way white privilege persists even in the context of diversity efforts.*

Although Mr. Carbondale's *intent* to be culturally sensitive and to bring the students together was genuine, the *impact* of the Diverse Friends Day activity was to sabotage the self-segregation decisions made by the students of color and to impose on the students' choice to sit together in the cafeteria. For those students, their choice is a coping strategy necessary for self-preservation (Tatum, 2017) and well-being. However, their choice is not antithetical to inclusionary practices that require the real work of the collective to affirm members of the learning community for who they are and how they work interdependently. We must be mindful that the collective includes our students. It wasn't sufficient for Mr. Carbondale to attend the Inclusion Excellence conference alone and work in isolation from the collective. The Diverse Friends Day activity was designed to force people to interact. These types of activities are top-down methods instead of collective alignments. To bring people together, we must take into consideration the deeper levels of culture and the need for high levels of emotional trust when building a culturally fortifying and sustaining organization.

Summary

Creating relational trust requires a common commitment to benevolence, reliability, competence, honesty, and openness. Collective communities depend upon each other and know that success and achieving their purpose is not an individual event. Organizations thrive on the stimuli that propel them forward, focusing on the matters of the heart directed toward every member of the learning community. This focus generates a motivation that fuels the commitment of coming together to create transformative equitable learning environments that interrupt systems of inequities. As we foster relational trust and strengthen our intrinsic motivation, there is a significant impact on the commitment of the learning community to cultivate long-lasting systems of inclusion, care, and shared accountability toward collective equity.

Chapter Highlights

- Many theorists on motivation, such as Maslow and Pink, focus on personal or individual factors that motivate humans.

- In a collectivist environment, humans are motivated by the whole instead of the part and emphasize the needs and goals of the group over the needs and desires of each individual.

- "Trust is an individual's or group's willingness to be vulnerable to another party based on the confidence that the latter party is benevolent, reliable, competent, honest, humble, and open." (Hoy & Tschannen-Moran, 1999, p. 189).

- Bryk and Schneider (2002) describe relational trust as a social phenomenon that is manifested by the shared perceptions and beliefs of the role groups in the school community. Relational trust emerges in the discernment of intentions, beliefs, and actions of the organization.

- In a collective, relational trust emerges from authentic interactions in the relational networks of a school (teacher-parent, principal-teacher, teacher-teacher, teacher-student, student-student, school-community

- "The circle of trust approach is distinguished by principles and practices intended to create a process of shared exploration where people can find a safe space to nurture personal and professional integrity and the courage to act on it" (Palmer, 2004).

- "Relational trust is built on movements of the human heart such as empathy, commitment, compassion, patience and the capacity to forgive" (Palmer, 2012).

- Palmer's movements of the human heart build relational trust in organizations. These are the stimuli of building relational trust that keep the collective motivated and focused on the work of transforming environments for the benefit of all.

- According to Daniel Pink (2009), motivation has three components: activation, persistence and intensity.

- In collective learning communities, the members share the accountability for nurturing one another.

- We must take into consideration the deeper levels of culture and the need for high levels of emotional trust when building a culturally fortifying and sustaining organization, and understand that these actions generate our *impact* regardless of our *intent*.

Invitation to Collective Thinking

- How will we create relational trust among the members of our collective?

- How would a learning community use the stimuli of building relational trust?

- What are some intrinsic factors that will motivate the learning community?

- How do you get members of the organization to realize that there is a distinction between impact and intent?

Reflection

The Cultural Consciousness Matrix below outlines the levels of knowing that empower a collective to bridge the knowing-doing gap.

THE CULTURAL CONSCIOUSNESS MATRIX	
Level 2	Level 3
Consciously Unskilled	Consciously Skilled
• You know that you don't know	• You know that you have the skill
• Beginning of growth	• Comfortable with being uncomfortable
• Crisis of consciousness	• Focused confidence
• Enlightened	• Intentional
Being	**Becoming**

(Continued)

(Continued)

Level 1	Level 4
Unconsciously Unskilled	Unconsciously Skilled
• You don't know what you don't know	• You know the skill and the skill is second nature
• Complete lack of knowledge and skills	• Completely confident
• Fixed mindset	• Automaticity, accountability, humility
• Oblivious	• Graceful
Existing	**Evolving**

Source: Adapted from Burch (1970).

In what ways has the information in Chapter 3 closed your knowing-doing gap?

_____

_____

_____

_____

What is your knowing-doing gap?

_____

_____

_____

_____

So what does this mean to you?

_____

_____

_____

_____

Now what are your immediate actions?

_____

_____

_____

Culturally Fortifying Practices

4

Strengthening All the Members in the Learning Community

//

Do the best you can until you know better. Then when you know better, do better.

—Maya Angelou

Just as we work to create conditions in which adults work together to create a culture that provides opportunities for every professional to thrive and to be recognized for who they are and the unique assets they bring to the collective, we work to create environments in which all students can show up in the fullness of who they are as learners. This is the essence of **culturally fortifying practices**. When the members of the collective are fortified for who they are, *they see, they hear, and they feel* themselves in every aspect of the school culture.

Fortification allows us to celebrate and sustain identities and differences by honoring and uplifting individuals in the learning community. Fortification increases levels of behavioral, cognitive, and emotional engagement. In culturally fortified classrooms, we intentionally lower our students' affective filters in a manner that allows all learners to learn. If students experience a lack of self-confidence, learning anxiety, and/or feelings of isolation, an imaginary wall (the affective filter) is built as a defense mechanism to protect their identities. According to Stephen Krashen's theory of second language acquisition, when the affective filter is low, an emotionally safe space for learning is created (Taylor Tricomi, 1986). Educators have the power to either lower or raise the affective filter of our students. When our students feel that they don't belong in our classrooms and schools, their affective filters are raised. "The brain takes its social needs very seriously and is fierce in protecting an individual's sense of well-being, self-determination, self-worth along with its connection to community. We cannot downplay students' need to feel safe and valued in the classroom" (Hammond, 2015, p. 47).

When students are empowered to wholeheartedly show up, the brain is ready for learning. Through cognitive engagement, they become invested in the learning process and are prepared to seek challenges and self-regulate in their classroom interactions. Emotional engagement is the bedrock for an intrinsic sense of belonging, all of which stimulates and sustains positive relationships and the desire to show up. "People become 'good at life' when they feel safe, valued and have a sense of purpose and meaning" (Fullan, 2021, p. 15). We become strong, we become brave, and *we can breathe.*

Without fortification, we lose the benefits of the connection we gain from being a collective. When we share a sense of reciprocity and genuine concern for one another's cultural, emotional, intellectual, and relational needs, we share a sense of belonging and strength. We are secure in our own intersecting identities and we honor the identities of others. Humans need to experience a sense of belonging within a community. Fortification benefits the essence of each individual in the collective. "Understanding this dichotomy is important to building a climate in which individuals from collective cultures can function and perceive that they are a part of the learning community" (Shade, Kelly, & Oberg, 1997, p. 56). If there is no value to the individual, it stands to reason that there is no benefit to the collective.

 Collective Equity Voices

Principal Joi Kilpatrick's Journey to Collective Equity

Principal Joi Kilpatrick started her equity journey in the DeKalb County School District as a 4th-grade teacher. As one of four Black teachers at her school, Joi felt the need to provide experiences to connect each individual student to the classroom community. Although the school was in an affluent area, many of her students resided in subsidized apartment complexes close to the school. She spent many years being an inclusive, culturally fortifying teacher by creating lessons that captivated all students as she built bridges to close equity gaps that existed among her students. Joi spent endless hours being a strong presence in the social and emotional lives of her students. She often attended extracurricular events such as baseball games, school parties, and other student functions that were not mandatory for staff. This was important in order to build significant relationships with her students and the school community. Joi continued her equity journey as an assistant principal in an elementary school serving primarily Latinx students. As a Black woman, she fought to ensure that all children, despite race, economic background, or any identity differences, would receive a world-class education. Joi did this by working closely with teachers to analyze data, creating professional development opportunities that increased cultural awareness, and modeling being a beacon of hope for equitable change. After several years of this continuous and rewarding work, Joi furthered her reach by becoming a principal in the Atlanta Public School District, serving economically disadvantaged students living in underserved communities.

During her tenure, Principal Kilpatrick has continued to provide an equitable learning environment for both students and staff. One of her first priorities was focusing on the data to identify equity gaps and to determine patterns of inequities. This analysis enabled the leadership team to identify professional learning to support teacher practice. Principal Kilpatrick implemented weekly data meetings with the professional learning community to diagnose and prescribe practices based upon the individual strengths and needs of students. Lessons that teachers created during their weekly professional learning communities included culturally relevant practices that reflected the student population. Principal Kilpatrick provided weekly professional learning sessions that were driven by the needed skills identified through the data analysis in the weekly teacher meetings. In these professional interactions, Kilpatrick didn't position herself as "the keeper of learning"; rather, she believed in teachers sharing their collective knowledge to create a thriving learning community.

Principal Kilpatrick's next major priority was extending her students experiences by providing a variety of learning options in the Arts. She offered a new Spanish class to not only promote Spanish language development, but to expose her students to the variety of cultures within the Latin community. She carved out time for students to attend general music, art, band, physical education, and dance. This provided students with opportunities that shaped and enhanced their cultural representations. In addition, the school provided a STEM lab that students attend at least once a week, which exposes them to rigor and critical thinking in complex disciplines. Finally, she also ensured that each day starts with a social-emotional learning lesson to develop students' skills in self-awareness, self-management, and self-regulation.

(Continued)

(Continued)

Realizing collective equity in action:

What are some examples of how Principal Kilpatrick fortified members of the learning community in her various roles?

What connections can you make between Principal Kilpatrick's journey and realizing collective equity in action?

_____

_____

_____

From Equity Moves to Culturally Fortifying Transformational Practices

A culturally fortified learning environment requires its members to routinely implement equity moves that are immediate, accessible, and relatable (see Figure 4.1). An **equity move** is a plan of action to mitigate inequities, disparities, stereotypes, biased mindsets, oppressive policies, and exclusionary systems by incorporating high-yield evidence-based practices that culturally fortify members of the learning community. Equity moves open the doors to all members feeling valued, seen, heard, validated, loved, understood, and cared for.

FIGURE 4.1   Equity Moves

IMMEDIATE	Act with urgency and agency
ACCESSIBLE	Act proactively instead of reactively
RELATABLE	Build relationships that add value to one another

Jot Thought

Equity Moves

How might equity moves that are immediate, accessible, and relatable fortify the learning environment?

_____

_____

_____

What are the implications of implementing equity moves?

_____

_____

_____

Give an example of how you would use an equity move to establish
a culturally fortifying environment.

_____

_____

_____

online
resources   Available for download from resources.corwin.com/CollectiveEquity

There are systemic practices that culturally fortify all members in the learning community when done with intention and design. Figure 4.2 represents four culturally fortifying practices of school transformation: organizational, curricular, instructional, and programmatic. Each practice is unpacked to show how the collective can design transformative equitable learning environments.

> Every student deserves a great teacher, not by chance but by design.
>
> —Fisher, Frey, and Hattie (2016)

Organizational Policies and Practices

Many internal change agents—adults and students—see education as the vehicle by which equity, excellence, and well-being can be achieved synergistically (Fullan & Gallagher, 2020). The collective is fortified through policies and practices that benefit all members regardless of their dimensions of identity. These include decisions and actions related to staffing and placement, professional learning, master scheduling, family and community partnerships, resourcing, aesthetics of the building, and disciplinary policies. In formulating and implementing our policies and practice, we must maintain an intentional and relentless focus on equity. Conversely, we must continue to act against the inequities that negatively impact the well-being of the collective to ensure that our practices are culturally fortifying. Although there are other culturally fortifying organizational policies and practices, in Figure 4.3 (see page 100), we identified those common to all learning communities.

FIGURE 4.2   School Transformation Practices

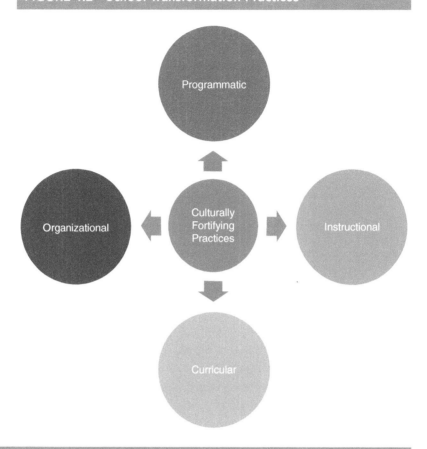

FIGURE 4.3   Organizational Practices That Are Culturally Fortifying

PRACTICES	STRATEGIES
Staffing and Placement	• Align staff and student cultural identities. • Choose staff members who have the capacity and willingness to create culturally empowering environments. • Base staff placement decisions on expertise instead of experience. • Focus attention on strategies to build staff agency, create respectful and supportive working environments, and establish opportunities to elevate voice and interest in order to reduce teacher turnover.
Professional Learning	• Align professional development to school equity goals and/or standards. • Continuously learn about implicit bias and other barriers to equitable practice, with attention to addressing biased mindsets in the learning community. • Set professional learning goals related to culturally fortifying practices. • Craft learning opportunities that are related to diversity, equity, culturally fortifying practices, and addressing disproportionalities. • Deploy an ongoing plan to monitor the impact of the learning opportunities; the improvement in knowledge, attitudes, and skills; and the organization's cultural humility.

PRACTICES	STRATEGIES
Master Schedules	• Base teacher assignments on the interdependence of the strengths of the teachers and the goals of the students. • Ensure the master schedule represents the unique needs, interests, aspirations, and skills of the entire learning community and the resources available to support them. • Build opportunities for consistent collaborative conversations around curriculum, instruction, and assessment to determine who is benefitting and who is not.
Family and Community Partnerships	• Continuously learn from and leverage the funds of knowledge of students and families. • Nurture and foster relationships within the families and communities to empower members to be involved, informed, and active in learning experiences. • Design structures in which dynamic family and community partnerships work collaboratively in the best interests of students. • Remain persistent in identifying the particular interests, aspirations, values, unique needs, skills, and challenges that impact family engagement.
Resourcing	• Utilize resource levers (people, time, and money) by spending more on students who face greater challenges in order to accelerate student learning and enhance engagement across dimensions of identities. • Position our expert teachers (Hattie, 2012) who are culturally fortifying and knowledgeable in the service of our most marginalized students. • Organize opportunities for collaborative structures that emphasize and promote the well-being of all members of the learning community. • Measure the impact of strategic resourcing on the mission, vision, and goals of creating transformative, equitable learning environments. • Use reliable measures and tools to assess the curriculum and assess for biases.
Climate and Culture	• Identify current realities that prevent the learning community from coming together to focus on shared values, individual assets, and equity of voices. • Create shared values that strengthen the school-life experiences for all by cultivating a sense of urgency to dismantle systems of inequities and practices that perpetuate stereotypes and biased mindsets. • Collect observational data on practices that foster collective, culturally relevant thinking and actions that enhance all aspects of the learning community.
Disciplinary Policies	• Identify root causes that contribute to inequities in discipline practices. • Eliminate punitive structures that exclude students from the learning community, which results in "prison to pipeline" manifestations that directly and indirectly push students of color out of school. • Implement restorative practices, act upon teachable moments, and reinforce the value of self-regulation in order to repair relationships, foster personal reflection, strengthen a sense of belonging, and reclaim community.

Shared Experience

Describe how your collective uses these organizational practices and strategies to fortify the learning community.

PRACTICES	STRATEGIES	CULTURALLY FORTIFYING ORGANIZATION PRACTICES AND STRATEGIES
Staffing and Placement	• Align staff and student cultural identities. • Choose staff members who have the capacity and willingness to create culturally empowering environments. • Base staff placement decisions on expertise instead of experience. • Focus attention on strategies to build staff agency, create respectful and supportive working environments, and establish opportunities to elevate voice and interest in order to reduce teacher turnover.	
Professional Learning	• Align professional development to school equity goals and/or standards. • Continuously learn about implicit bias and other barriers to equitable practice, with attention to addressing biased mindsets in the learning community. • Set professional learning goals related to culturally fortifying practices. • Craft learning opportunities that are related to diversity, equity, culturally fortifying practices, and addressing disproportionalities. • Deploy an ongoing plan to monitor the impact of the learning opportunities; the improvement in knowledge, attitudes, and skills; and the organization's cultural humility.	
Master Schedules	• Base teacher assignments on the interdependence of the strengths of the teachers and the goals of the students. • Ensure the master schedule represents the unique needs, interests, aspirations, and skills of the entire learning community and the resources available to support them. • Build opportunities for consistent collaborative conversations around curriculum, instruction, and assessment to determine who is benefitting and who is not.	

PRACTICES	STRATEGIES	CULTURALLY FORTIFYING ORGANIZATION PRACTICES AND STRATEGIES
Family and Community Partnerships	• Continuously learn from and leverage the funds of knowledge of students and families. • Nurture and foster relationships within the families and communities to empower members to be involved, informed, and active in learning experiences. • Design structures in which dynamic family and community partnerships work collaboratively in the best interests of students. • Remain persistent in identifying the particular interests, aspirations, values, unique needs, skills, and challenges that impact family engagement.	
Resourcing	• Utilize resource levers (people, time, and money) by spending more on students who face greater challenges in order to accelerate student learning and enhance engagement across dimensions of identities. • Position our expert teachers (Hattie, 2012) who are culturally fortifying and knowledgeable in the service of our most marginalized students. • Organize opportunities for collaborative structures that emphasize and promote the well-being of all members of the learning community. • Measure the impact of strategic resourcing on the mission, vision, and goals of creating transformative, equitable learning environments. • Use reliable measures and tools to assess the curriculum and assess for biases.	
Climate and Culture	• Identify current realities that prevent the learning community from coming together to focus on shared values, individual assets, and equity of voices. • Create shared values that strengthen the school-life experiences for all by cultivating a sense of urgency to dismantle systems of inequities and practices that perpetuate stereotypes and biased mindsets. • Collect observational data on practices that foster collective, culturally relevant thinking and actions that enhance all aspects of the learning community.	

(Continued)

(Continued)

PRACTICES	STRATEGIES	CULTURALLY FORTIFYING ORGANIZATION PRACTICES AND STRATEGIES
Disciplinary Policies	• Identify root causes that contribute to inequities in discipline practices. • Eliminate punitive structures that exclude students from the learning community, which results in "prison to pipeline" manifestations that directly and indirectly push students of color out of school. • Implement restorative practices, act upon teachable moments, and reinforce the value of self-regulation in order to repair relationships, foster personal reflection, strengthen a sense of belonging, and reclaim community.	

 Available for download from resources.corwin.com/CollectiveEquity

 Shared Experience

Culturally Fortifying Organizational Practices Assessment

Using the Culturally Fortifying Organizational Practices Assessment below, identify where you are as a collective with implementing culturally fortifying practices. Once completed, discuss the implications for your learning community.

CULTURALLY FORTIFYING ORGANIZATIONAL PRACTICES	FREQUENCY OF USE			
	NEVER	RARELY	SOMETIMES	OFTEN
1. Our staff represents the dimensions of identity of our students.				
2. Our teaching staff represents the dimensions of identity of our students.				
3. Equity goals are aligned to our daily practice.				

CULTURALLY FORTIFYING ORGANIZATIONAL PRACTICES	FREQUENCY OF USE			
	NEVER	RARELY	SOMETIMES	OFTEN
4. Teachers and other learning community members can articulate the equity goals.				
5. Professional learning sessions align to equity goals.				
6. Professional learning provided for staff is steeped in culturally fortifying practices.				
7. Organizational policies, systems, procedures, and practices address inequities based on dimensions of identity.				
8. Organizational policies and practices provide all learners with appropriate access, exposure, and inclusion.				
9. Ongoing and appropriate monitoring and accountability measures are established to address inequities and equity gaps in teaching and learning.				
10. Teacher assignments are based on teaching strengths and the goals of the students.				
11. Teachers leverage teachable moments to strengthen community expectations, restoration of relationships, and the reinforcement of the value of self-regulation.				
12. We engage in ongoing, collaborative conversations around curriculum, instruction, and assessment based on who is benefitting and who is not benefitting.				
13. Funds, staff, and other resources are allotted based on the needs and identified equity gaps in order to ensure well-being, achievement, excellence, and the success of all members of the learning community.				
14. Incentives are provided to attract, retain, and sustain teachers who reflect the populations of the student body.				

(Continued)

(Continued)

CULTURALLY FORTIFYING ORGANIZATIONAL PRACTICES	FREQUENCY OF USE			
	NEVER	RARELY	SOMETIMES	OFTEN
15. Teams identify the forces that impede learning by the perpetuation of biased language, practices, and actions.				
16. Strategies are implemented to ensure adequate and equitable participation of all stakeholders in the resource allocation process.				
17. Teams implement practices and structures that restore students when behavioral challenges arise.				
18. Teams eliminate punitive structures that exclude students from the learning community.				
19. The school improvement plan reflects equity, access, exposure, expectations, and equitable practices for all members in the learning community.				
20. We actively and meaningfully engage families, parents, guardians, and caregivers of all groups of learners in order to support learners' success in school.				

 Available for download from resources.corwin.com/CollectiveEquity

Curricular Practices

Curriculum refers to planned learning experiences with intended outcomes that also recognize the importance of possible unintended outcomes. There are three distinct types of curriculum: the explicit curriculum (core curriculum), the hidden curriculum (unofficial curriculum), and the absent curriculum (intentionally or unintentionally excluded). The explicit curriculum serves as the roadmap for educators to determine what is essential to teaching and learning. It must ensure that all students, regardless of their dimensions of identity, have an opportunity to learn, have access to rigorous academic experiences, find relevance, and make connections to the content and materials. Every student must have access to a guaranteed and viable curriculum (Marzano, 2003). In the context of culturally fortified learning environments, *guaranteed* refers to giving students the opportunity to learn from a curriculum that is relevant and representative of their lived experiences. Viability ensures that students have the time, resources, and means to engage at the behavioral, cognitive, and emotional levels of learning. When there is a guaranteed and viable curriculum, students have access to the same knowledge and skills in schools across the learning community in a manner that disrupts the "those kids can't...." syndrome. Curricular practices that are culturally fortifying are listed in Figure 4.4.

FIGURE 4.4   Curricular Practices That Are Culturally Fortifying

PRACTICES	STRATEGIES
Assessment	• Gather and use information on students' learning to identify progress, gaps, and where to go next.
	• Use multiple strategies for students to demonstrate knowledge and skills in the learning process, such as compiling a self-directed portfolio of selected artifacts to show what they know.
	• Incorporate universal assessment strategies that allow you modify and adjust instruction for all learners.
	• Optimize information on student interests, prior knowledge, and feedback from the student to the teacher to design assessments anchored in culturally fortifying pedagogy.
Data Analysis	• Choose artifacts and keep conversations about equity and bias at the heart of the analysis process.
	• Personalize every data point with the realization that each source is connected to a student's story, lived experience, and internal brilliance that may be overlooked through traditional methods of assessment.
	• Observe, listen to, gather, and analyze artifacts from their lived experiences to discern information about students' academic experiences (Safir & Dugan, 2021).
	• Cultivate an asset-based process to strengthen the quality of the collaborative conversations that result in dismantling systemic stereotypes and barriers to learning.

(Continued)

FIGURE 4.4   (Continued)

PRACTICES	STRATEGIES
Standard Analysis	• Establish what all students need to know and be able to do and the depth of thinking required to create culturally responsive experiences. • Design the instructional flow to consider the current knowledge of all students and determine how the skills and concepts align to students' cultures and are relevant to their personal experiences. • Leverage the interdependence of the learning expectations and the ways in which they show up for learners.
Cultural Representations	• Find relevance to the students' personal interests, personalities, backgrounds, and dimensions of identity so they can connect to themselves, the learning community, the world around them, and the content. • Provide a variety of cultural perspectives and viewpoints in materials, examples, and experiences. • Build on students' individual cultures to enhance behavioral, cognitive, and emotional engagement.

 Shared Experience

Describe how your collective uses these curricular practices and strategies to fortify the learning community.

PRACTICES	STRATEGIES	CULTURALLY FORTIFYING ORGANIZATION PRACTICES AND STRATEGIES
Assessment	• Gather and use information on students' learning to identify progress, gaps, and where to go next. • Use multiple strategies for students to demonstrate knowledge and skills in the learning process, such as compiling a self-directed portfolio of selected artifacts to show what they know. • Incorporate universal assessment strategies that allow you modify and adjust instruction for all learners. • Optimize information on student interests, prior knowledge, and feedback from the student to the teacher to design assessments anchored in culturally fortifying pedagogy.	

PRACTICES	STRATEGIES	CULTURALLY FORTIFYING ORGANIZATION PRACTICES AND STRATEGIES
Data Analysis	• Choose artifacts and keep conversations about equity and bias at the heart of the analysis process. • Personalize every data point with the realization that each source is connected to a student's story, lived experience, and internal brilliance that may be overlooked through traditional methods of assessment. • Observe, listen to, gather, and analyze artifacts from their lived experiences to discern information about students' academic experiences (Safir & Dugan, 2021). • Cultivate an asset-based process to strengthen the quality of the collaborative conversations that result in dismantling systemic stereotypes and barriers to learning.	
Standard Analysis	• Establish what all students need to know and be able to do and the depth of thinking required to create culturally responsive experiences. • Design the instructional flow to consider the current knowledge of all students and determine how the skills and concepts align to students' cultures and are relevant to their personal experiences. • Leverage the interdependence of the learning expectations and the ways in which they show up for learners.	
Cultural Representations	• Find relevance to the students' personal interests, personalities, backgrounds, and dimensions of identity so they can connect to themselves, the learning community, the world around them, and the content. • Provide a variety of cultural perspectives and viewpoints in materials, examples, and experiences. • Build on students' individual cultures to enhance behavioral, cognitive, and emotional engagement.	

Shared Experience

Culturally Fortifying Curricular Practices Assessment

Using the Culturally Fortifying Curricular Practices Assessment below, identify where you are as a collective with implementing culturally fortifying practices. Once completed, discuss the implications for your learning community.

CULTURALLY FORTIFYING CURRICULAR PRACTICES	FREQUENCY OF USE			
	NEVER	RARELY	SOMETIMES	OFTEN
1. Related course materials are rich and relevant to the lived and cultural experiences of students.				
2. Materials incorporate cultural representations of the students and a variety of perspectives are elevated.				
3. To represent difficult content, materials incorporate metaphors that students understand based on their prior knowledge and lived experiences.				
4. Materials are void of messages that reinforce stereotypes or cultural bias.				
5. Materials omit and/or erase certain groups based on dimensions of identity, diverse perspectives, contributions, authentic accounts, and lived experiences.				
6. Materials include marginalizations of people based on social and cultural inequities.				
7. Materials depict BIPOC in subservient and passive roles.				
8. Materials depict white people in leadership and in powerful and privileged roles.				
9. Books portray characters that reinforce stereotypes. Books with Black characters are all about slavery, poverty, single moms, and/or sports; the books with Latin characters are about them being new to the United States and their "illegal" status, poverty, lack of drive, and gang affiliations; and books that include people with disabilities focus on their disability.				
10. Materials rarely reflect diversity in the curricula. When mirrors are provided, students see themselves presented as criminals, angry, slaves, victims, malicious, pitied, or through an otherwise deficit lens.				
11. How often are texts and media sources updated?				

CULTURALLY FORTIFYING CURRICULAR PRACTICES	FREQUENCY OF USE			
	NEVER	RARELY	SOMETIMES	OFTEN
12. Diverse student perspectives are presented in materials in mostly significant and positive ways.				
13. When characters from diverse dimensions of identity are represented, they are admired because of how they are subservient to those in power.				
14. When characters from diverse dimensions of identity are represented, they are held in as high regard as other characters because of qualities associated with the dominant culture, such as courage, perseverance, strength, determination, kindness, generosity, and intelligence.				
15. We check for bias, stereotypes, negative mental models, inaccuracy, and inappropriateness in the depiction of specific cultures and social groups that are represented in our materials.				
16. We examine the cultural representation of individuals with unique characteristics, aspirations, abilities, language styles, strengths, weaknesses, interests, values, goals, and lived experiences vs. depictions of negativity and deficit-based beliefs about groups of people.				
17. We look for the "single stories" that reinforce and perpetuate biases, marginalizations, and stereotypes about a group of people.				
18. Materials provide scaffolds and multiple entry points for students to build their understanding of complex, rigorous, diverse perspectives and uncommon and new experiences.				
19. Materials communicate positive depictions and experiences of different cultural groups.				
20. Materials include "mirrors" in which students can see themselves and their cultures represented. The **mirror opportunities** can provide three levels of relevance: personal association, personal usefulness, and personal identification.				
21. Materials include "windows" into the authentic experiences of different people and their diverse cultures. When **window opportunities** are taught with conviction and intentionality, students will develop a greater awareness of other cultures and dimensions of identity.				

Instructional Practices

Creating equitable educational opportunities for all has been an espoused goal of American educational policy since 1954 (Blackmore, 2009). But history has demonstrated that achieving it will take more than legislation (Orfield & Eaton, 1996). What will it take? What do we need to consider? How are educational opportunities for all students being represented in the classroom? How has history informed how we teach? We must call out and address the inequities and biases that continue to perpetuate oppressive learning cultures. We must also be aware when we have missed the mark and be willing to interrupt the ways in which we don't engage and don't respond to dimensions of identity or have intentionally or unintentionally created an uninviting learning environment (Purkey & Novak, 2015). When creating culturally fortifying learning environments, instructional practices are the catalyst for students showing up ready, empowered, and motivated to learn.

To create such environments, teachers use methods that foster personal connections, personal usefulness, and personal identifications to draw students into the learning process (see Figure 4.5). This methodology is culturally relevant teaching, a concept that originated with researcher Gloria Ladson-Billings (1995), who defines it as "a pedagogy that empowers students intellectually, socially, emotionally, and politically by using cultural referents to impart knowledge, skills, and attitudes." Geneva Gay (2010) further explains that culturally responsive teaching "uses the cultural knowledge, prior experiences, frames of reference, and performance styles of ethnically diverse students to make learning more relevant and effective." Culturally responsive practices break down barriers and strengthen engagement for historically marginalized learners. They stimulate the emotional, cultural, and intellectual development of all members in the learning community. The intent of cultural fortification is to strengthen and sustain cultural representations based upon Hammond's Three Levels of Culture (see Chapter 1). When there is a fortification, we open students' eyes to new perspectives, diverse ways of thinking, the multitude of values in society, and realms of possibilities.

 Jot Thought

What Will It Take?

What will it take to create equitable educational opportunities for all?

_____

_____

_____

_____

What do we need to consider for this to happen?

_____

_____

_____

_____

How are educational opportunities for all students being represented in the classroom?

_____

_____

_____

_____

How has history defined who we are instructionally?

_____

_____

_____

_____

online resources   Available for download from resources.corwin.com/CollectiveEquity

Programmatic Practices

We share a responsibility for promoting educational excellence across the entire learning community. Programmatic structures counter reactionary practices that minimize who students are as learners and their capacity for learning. In particular, we must move beyond outmoded models of schooling to personalized learning environments that focus on what students need as individuals. These needs include an array of cognitive, emotional, cultural, and behavioral variables. Programmatic practices are foundational in designing a cyclical process of instructing, accelerating, engaging, and assessing what students need to strengthen their capacity to thrive as individual learners. For example, actions

FIGURE 4.5   Instructional Practices That Are Culturally Fortifying

PRACTICES	STRATEGIES
Teacher Clarity	• Identify relevance in what students need to know and be able to do to ensure increased engagement and motivation. • Create student-centered learning experiences that allow for self-regulation throughout the learning process. • Establish a continuous process that supports identification of individual student mastery of the standards. • Provide access and exposure to success criteria that align to the skills and concepts that students need to master.
Deliberate Design	• Shift the focus from the teacher to thinking about learners first and what they need academically and emotionally in order to create a sense of belonging and connectedness to the instructional process. • Utilize instructional resources that focus on who the students are and empower them to demonstrate what they know, how they think, and methods to reach them in all phases of learning. • Foster student collaboration and create active learning environments that reflect various entry points, students' interests, learning preferences, and ways in which they process information. • Create instructional spaces that increase behavioral, cognitive, and emotional engagement to intentionally elevate students' self-efficacy and self-confidence.
Cultural Bridges	• Integrate affirmations, create community agreements, and ensure trust is maintained throughout the learning process. • Act as a cultural liaison, teach from the heart, develop connections to the cultures of the students, and create learning partnerships with members of the class community. • Recognize the tenets of the Levels of Culture and assess what actions have an intense emotional impact of trust.
Engagement Strategies	• Balance cognitive demand with the conditions of care and personal regard. • Create emotional connections so learners experience safe academic spaces in order to take risks throughout the learning process. • Expose students to current content to cultivate relevance to the "societal curriculum". • Establish ways of learning that are natural and inclusive of strategies that are visual, multisensory, conversational, student-generated, and connected to students' cultural realities.

such as the following create access to programs that help students realize their potential:

• Offering culturally inclusive sports options

• Placing cultural representation into programmatic identification processes

Shared Experience

Describe how your collective uses these instructional practices and strategies to fortify the learning community.

PRACTICES	STRATEGIES	CULTURALLY FORTIFYING ORGANIZATION PRACTICES AND STRATEGIES
Teacher Clarity	• Identify relevance in what students need to know and be able to do to ensure increased engagement and motivation. • Create student-centered learning experiences that allow for self-regulation throughout the learning process. • Establish a continuous process that supports identification of individual student mastery of the standards. • Provide access and exposure to success criteria that align to the skills and concepts that students need to master.	
Deliberate Design	• Shift the focus from the teacher to thinking about learners first and what they need academically and emotionally in order to create a sense of belonging and connectedness to the instructional process. • Utilize instructional resources that focus on who the students are and empower them to demonstrate what they know, how they think, and methods to reach them in all phases of learning. • Foster student collaboration and create active learning environments that reflect various entry points, students' interests, learning preferences, and ways in which they process information. • Create instructional spaces that increase behavioral, cognitive, and emotional engagement to intentionally elevate students' self-efficacy and self-confidence.	
Cultural Bridges	• Integrate affirmations, create community agreements, and ensure trust is maintained throughout the learning process. • Act as a cultural liaison, teach from the heart, develop connections to the cultures of the students, and create learning partnerships with members of the class community. • Recognize the tenets of the Levels of Culture and assess what actions have an intense emotional impact of trust.	

(Continued)

(Continued)

PRACTICES	STRATEGIES	CULTURALLY FORTIFYING ORGANIZATION PRACTICES AND STRATEGIES
Engagement Strategies	• Balance cognitive demand with the conditions of care and personal regard. • Create emotional connections so learners experience safe academic spaces in order to take risks throughout the learning process. • Expose students to current content to cultivate relevance to the "societal curriculum". • Establish ways of learning that are natural and inclusive of strategies that are visual, multisensory, conversational, student-generated, and connected to students' cultural realities.	

 Available for download from resources.corwin.com/CollectiveEquity

 Shared Experience

Culturally Fortifying Instructional Practices Assessment

Using the Culturally Fortifying Instructional Practices Assessment below, identify where you are as a collective with implementing culturally fortifying practices. Once completed, discuss the implications for your learning community.

CULTURALLY FORTIFYING INSTRUCTIONAL PRACTICES	FREQUENCY OF USE			
	NEVER	RARELY	SOMETIMES	OFTEN
1. Teachers create an environment of warmth by greeting students by name and pronouncing their names correctly.				
2. Teachers show an interest in their students by providing an opportunity for students to share their voices.				
3. Teachers use immediacy with all students by circling around the room to easily interact with students.				

CULTURALLY FORTIFYING INSTRUCTIONAL PRACTICES	FREQUENCY OF USE			
	NEVER	RARELY	SOMETIMES	OFTEN
4. Teachers align instructional resources with cultural representations of students.				
5. Teachers provide students with opportunities to learn about themselves and their problem-solving skills.				
6. Teachers are deliberate in supporting *all* students with academic rigor by using and losing scaffolds.				
7. Teachers use curriculum, books, learning strategies, demonstrations, audio, and visual materials that connect to individual identities and cultural representations.				
8. Teachers use varied data sources to direct instruction.				
9. Teachers provide students with opportunities to learn about others and their perspectives.				
10. Teachers model expectations so there is student understanding, agreement, and commitment to shared community expectations.				
11. Teachers leverage teachable moments to strengthen community expectations, restoration of relationships, and the reinforcement of the value of self-regulation.				
12. Teachers ask higher order questions equitably of all students.				
13. Teachers provide clarity by communicating learning intentions and success criteria.				
14. Teachers create an environment of respect, consistency, and shared power in order to develop social and relational skills among the class.				
15. Teachers incorporate relevant content that is applicable outside the classroom.				
16. Teachers provide feedback that is growth producing by identifying what students need to start, continue, and tweak.				

(Continued)

(Continued)

CULTURALLY FORTIFYING INSTRUCTIONAL PRACTICES	FREQUENCY OF USE			
	NEVER	RARELY	SOMETIMES	OFTEN
17. Teachers cultivate opportunities for all students to listen, speak, read, write, and think about the content.				
18. Teachers hold individual conversations with students to help them identify their strengths, needs, and goals.				
19. Teachers build choice and voice into tasks, assignments, and projects so students can self-regulate and own their learning.				
20. Teachers foster classroom discussions prompted by questions that open up student thinking and give them the space to share their ideas.				

- Eliminating disproportionality and ensuring entry into gifted and talented programs, including critically examining the criteria for such programs and ensuring that they are free from bias

- Giving all students an opportunity to qualify for extracurricular activities

- Using differentiated models to ensure cultural relevance to all students

In order to attain this goal, the learning community must commit to offering programs that are uniquely tailored to students' strengths and needs. When we analyze response to intervention in culturally relevant ways, we heighten our awareness of the lived experiences of marginalized students and encourage educators to consider perspectives beyond their own that promote rigor, relevance, and relationships (Ladson-Billings, 1995). Learning communities that reinforce cultural relevance enhance extracurricular activities, relentlessly engage and involve families, and purposefully design services that value and support individual learning processes (see Figure 4.6).

FIGURE 4.6 Programmatic Practices That Are Culturally Fortifying

PRACTICES	STRATEGIES
Culturally Relevant Response to Intervention	• Identify the causes of the barriers that create and perpetuate lack of progress, engagement, and achievement.
	• Provide intensive supports and scaffolds that offer access and exposure to students who do not respond to the core instruction, are not mastering the standards, or are not making the expected gains in learning.
	• Remove barriers based on unique learning needs; monitor progress and collect ongoing evidence of learning through assessments.
	• Build the capacity of the learning community to align instruction to grade-level outcomes and students' cultural connections to vary instruction and respond to the academic, emotional, behavioral, and cultural needs of learners.
	• Ensure that when students don't respond to classroom interventions, there is a system of intense acceleration to build upon current knowledge and skills that provides supplemental and tailored opportunities for learning.
Gifted and Talented	• Embed inclusionary practices at initial levels of identification of academic potential for gifted and talented programs.
	• Include universal screening methods to level the playing field and provide equal access and considerations for under-identified students.
	• Acknowledge unique learning needs and preferences and bolster culturally relevant pedagogy to connect with all dimensions of identity.
Extracurricular Activities	• Provide equal access to opportunities to develop life skills such as communication, collaboration, stewardship, time management, problem solving, adaptability, flexibility, resilience, active listening, and intentional participation.
	• Ask students what kind of activities appeal to them and create offerings to meet those interests.
	• Ensure that resources such as time, money, family commitments, and work schedules as well as language differences are not barriers to participation.
Parent Involvement and Engagement	• Strengthen family partnerships by building relational trust, sharing knowledge and power, and increasing communication among all families, students and educators.
	• Communicate to students and families that cultural identities are understood, acknowledged, and valued by intentionally providing a range of opportunities that reach families where they are and consider their needs and interests.
	• Bridge language differences by using translators when needed.
	• Convey the desire to include equity of voice.
Special Services	• Ensure all learners are identified using accurate data sources and intentionally provide targeted instruction to accelerate learning.
	• Provide access to core instruction with immediate and specific scaffolds and supports.
	• Disrupt the fossilization of academic growth by developing assets-based mindsets, cultivating individual ownership of goals, creating collaborative engagement opportunities, and building motivation for agency.

Shared Experience

Describe how your collective uses these programmatic practices and strategies to fortify the learning community.

PRACTICES	STRATEGIES	CULTURALLY FORTIFYING ORGANIZATION PRACTICES AND STRATEGIES
Culturally Relevant Response to Intervention	• Identify the causes of the barriers that create and perpetuate lack of progress, engagement, and achievement. • Provide intensive supports and scaffolds that offer access and exposure to students who do not respond to the core instruction, are not mastering the standards, or are not making the expected gains in learning. • Remove barriers based on unique learning needs; monitor progress and collect ongoing evidence of learning through assessments. • Build the capacity of the learning community to align instruction to grade-level outcomes and students' cultural connections to vary instruction and respond to the academic, emotional, behavioral, and cultural needs of learners. • Ensure that when students don't respond to classroom interventions, there is a system of intense acceleration to build upon current knowledge and skills that provides supplemental and tailored opportunities for learning.	
Gifted and Talented	• Embed inclusionary practices at initial levels of identification of academic potential for gifted and talented programs. • Include universal screening methods to level the playing field and provide equal access and considerations for under-identified students. • Acknowledge unique learning needs and preferences and bolster culturally relevant pedagogy to connect with all dimensions of identity.	

PRACTICES	STRATEGIES	CULTURALLY FORTIFYING ORGANIZATION PRACTICES AND STRATEGIES
Extracurricular Activities	• Provide equal access to opportunities to develop life skills such as communication, collaboration, stewardship, time management, problem solving, adaptability, flexibility, resilience, active listening, and intentional participation. • Ask students what kind of activities appeal to them and create offerings to meet those interests. • Ensure that resources such as time, money, family commitments, and work schedules as well as language differences are not barriers to participation.	
Parent Involvement and Engagement	• Strengthen family partnerships by building relational trust, sharing knowledge and power, and increasing communication. among all families, students and educators. • Communicate to students and families that cultural identities are understood, acknowledged, and valued by intentionally providing a range of opportunities that reach families where they are and consider their needs and interests. • Bridge language differences by using translators when needed. • Convey the desire to include equity of voice.	
Special Services	• Ensure all learners are identified using accurate data sources and intentionally provide targeted instruction to accelerate learning. • Provide access to core instruction with immediate and specific scaffolds and supports. • Disrupt the fossilization of academic growth by developing assets-based mindsets, cultivating individual ownership of goals, creating collaborative engagement opportunities, and building motivation for agency.	

Shared Experience

Culturally Fortifying Programmatic Practices Assessment

Using the Culturally Fortifying Programmatic Practices Assessment below, identify where you are as a collective with implementing culturally fortifying practices. Once completed, discuss the implications for your learning community.

CULTURALLY FORTIFYING PROGRAMMATIC PRACTICES	FREQUENCY OF USE			
	NEVER	RARELY	SOMETIMES	OFTEN
1. Intensive supports are provided to students who do not respond to core instruction.				
2. We remove barriers to achievement, well-being, and success for all students.				
3. There are high achievement expectations and outcomes for all learners.				
4. Science, literacy, numeracy, world languages, social studies, and digital competency are afforded to all students regardless of their dimensions of identity.				
5. Extracurricular activities appeal to all students' interests.				
6. Students have voice and input in the creation of programs and extracurricular activities.				
7. Resources are not a barrier to student participation in our programs.				
8. Family partnerships are built on relational trust, sharing of knowledge and power.				
9. Ongoing communication structures are established to address inequities and equity gaps in the learning community.				
10. Programs for high ability are inclusive of all dimensions of identity.				
11. Programs for special education are inclusive of all dimensions of identity.				

CULTURALLY FORTIFYING PROGRAMMATIC PRACTICES	FREQUENCY OF USE			
	NEVER	RARELY	SOMETIMES	OFTEN
12. Our instructional programs emphasize acceleration and not remediation.				
13. Funds and resources are allotted to programs that are reflective of the students and families in our learning community.				
14. Programs reflect rigor, relevance, and a focus on deepening relationships.				
15. Programs are created and implemented for decreasing isolation, exclusion, and segregation of culturally and racially diverse students.				
16. Academic and social-emotional well-being of all is at the very core of what we do in our learning community.				
17. We equitably incorporate counseling strategies and programs that enhance opportunities for all learners.				
18. School-parent-community learning partnerships exist and foster full access, inclusion, equitable experiences, and meaningful engagement for parents and community members.				
19. The school improvement plan reflects equitable programming and inclusive opportunities for all learning community members.				
20. We create and value ongoing conversations focusing on equitable programming with all members in our school and the community.				
21. Our ongoing conversations focusing on equitable opportunities lead to designing specific programs.				

Read the narrative below and engage in the **Jot Thought** to tap into your inner experience using your knowledge of creating culturally fortifying learning communities.

Let's consider Abdu, for example. He is a bright young man who entered our school in 7th grade after having struggled in previous schools and being removed from one school after another. His older brother had experienced success at our school, so Abdu came to us. He was opposed to this. He didn't want to know staff or build relationships with anybody. He wanted to do his own thing, his own way.

A few days after enrolling, Abdu decided to pull the fire alarm inside our building, sending the entire school into evacuation mode and automatically alerting the fire department. When we found out Abdu had done this, Dominique, an administrator, met with him to have a conversation. This first thing Abdu said was, "How long am I suspended?" This caught Dominique by surprise; he was not used to having this kind of conversation include talk of suspension.

He paused just a moment, then asked Abdu, "How do you like the school?" Now it was Abdu's turn to be surprised. "What do you mean, 'how do I like school'?" he shot back. Dominique persisted. "How do you like this school?" he asked. Abdu gave a typical 7th grader's response; "It's cool, I guess." But the questions from Dominique continued: "Why did you choose this school?" "What class have you enjoyed the most?" How has your day been today?"

It was clear that Abdu was starting of feel confused, because there had been no questions about the fire alarm, but he answered the questions put to him. He'd gotten in trouble and his parents had chosen this school, not him. He enjoyed history the best. His day was bad.

Dominique saw an opportunity he'd been looking for. "Why is your day bad?" he asked. Again, Abdu looked up with confusion. "It's bad because my dad left and isn't coming home for six months," he said. The tough 7th grader had let his mask slip a little, giving his administrator a look at the hurt kid behind it.

"I'm sorry that you're hurting," Dominque said. "Did that play into the situation today?" Abdu looked up again, realizing that finally, here was the fire alarm question he'd been expecting, "Yeah," he said. "I wanted to get caught. I wanted you to call home. I wanted to talk to my dad, and I knew my mom would call him if I got in trouble."

The conversation continued from there. Dominique went on to inform Abdu that the decision he'd mad wasn't a smart one and wasn't his best choice. He added that he understood Abdu was just trying to be heard, trying to use his voice. "If you want to talk to your dad, Abdu, I'll figure out a way to help."

"Are you calling my mom?" Abdu asked. Dominique replied that he wouldn't because he didn't want his first conversation with Abdu's mother to be a negative one. He then explained that he wanted Abdu to be able to own this poor choice and to make things right with his classmates. Abdu agreed and said he wanted to apologize to each class and be able to move forward. Dominique agreed to help him make these apologies. As they walked out of the office, Abdu stopped, looked at Dominique and said, "Thanks. No one has ever heard my voice before."

This is one example of how an administrator took the time to build a relationship with a student. The entire point of the exchange was to get Abdu back into a learning environment and keep the problematic behavior from happening again. The next day, Abdu's mother came to school. She was very apologetic, saying, "I'll pay the fine for the false fire alarm, and you can suspend him, but please don't kick him out of your school. It's the first time that *he* came to tell me what he did wrong instead of it being the school or police. "Not only did Abdu confess responsibility to his mom, he also carried through with his plan of asking forgiveness from every class for interrupting their learning.

Source: From *Building Equity: Policies and Practices to Empower All Learners*, D. Smith, N. Frey, I. Pumpian, D. Fisher, Alexandria, VA: ASCD, © 2017 by ASCD. Reprinted with permission. All rights reserved.

Jot Thought

Fortifying the Learning Community

What practices are evident in this immersive experience?

_____

_____

_____

(Continued)

(Continued)
What actions did the administrator engage in to fortify Abdu and his family in this immersive experience?

_____

_____

_____

 Available for download from resources.corwin.com/CollectiveEquity

Culturally Fortifying Classroom Strategies

There is a sense of urgency in education that requires us to commit to the work of equity while changing our hearts. This means we must commit to the journey while also committing to the work.

—Unknown

Culturally fortified environments are paramount in uplifting members of the learning community. These environments ensure that students are front and center in all facets of the educational process. As we create culturally fortified learning environments, we place the student at the heart of creating collective equity. Figure 4.7 lists culturally fortifying classroom strategies that elevate and enhance all students regardless of their dimensions of identity. These strategies mitigate the impact of inequities and stereotype threat.

FIGURE 4.7   A Checklist of Culturally Fortifying Classroom Strategies

Students are fortified in all the dimensions of engagement.

- ☐ Students see their culture and themselves through mirror opportunities (e.g., pictures, displays, artifacts, use of language, literature).
- ☐ Students have a positive sense of belonging.
- ☐ Time and space are provided for interest centers, inquiry, and exploratory learning styles.
- ☐ Students are given the learning tools and strategies to take risks, receive help, have more questions answered, and to express their creativity.

Students are fortified in their cultural representations.

- ☐ Teachers use the culture of their students as one way to strengthen learning dispositions, learning styles, and ways of engaging.
- ☐ Teachers build language bridges that provide students with opportunities to learn from and with each other as they grow and become cultural citizens.
- ☐ Students are affirmed by content, experiences, and collaborative structures that empower and give way to the intersectionalities of who they are as individuals.
- ☐ Teachers create an intentionally inviting learning environment where academic excellence, relational trust, and cultural identity are synonymous.

Students are fortified by deliberate instructional design.

☐ Teachers create an environment of high expectations of all students. Teachers build relational trust, resilience, interest, perseverance, and the motivation of students.

☐ Teachers utilize instructional resources that focus on who the students are, what they know, how they think, and how to reach them in all phases of learning.

☐ Academic rigor is for all and scaffolds are deliberate and aligned to learning.

☐ Teachers understand brain research and the relationships among cognitive, emotional, relational, and cultural learning processes.

Students are fortified by cultural bridges.

☐ Teachers recognize the tenets of the Levels of Culture, so there is an increase in emotional impact and the way students engage.

☐ Teachers use curriculum, books, learning strategies, demonstrations, audio, and visual materials in relevant ways; students experience connections to their individual identities and cultural representations.

☐ Teachers use varied data sources and disaggregate data by race, ethnicity, interest, language, class, and gender to direct their instruction.

☐ Teachers develop connections to the cultures of the students and create learning partnerships with members of the class community.

Students are fortified by disciplinary practices.

☐ Teachers model expectations so there is student understanding, agreement, and commitment to community expectations.

☐ Teachers leverage teachable moments to strengthen community expectations, restore relationships, and reinforce the value of self-regulation.

☐ Teachers create an environment of respect, consistency, and shared power from the onset to develop social and relational skills, making discipline educative rather than punitive.

☐ Teachers assist students in understanding the relationship between school expectations and school culture.

 Jot Thought

Fortifying the Learning Community

Within the learning community, the classroom is a major representation of the impact of creating transformative equitable learning environments. Identify how you can leverage one or more of the culturally fortifying

(Continued)

(Continued)
classroom strategies to mitigate inequities and address stereotypes in the classroom.

_____

_____

_____

_____

_____

_____

> Every student deserves a great teacher, not by chance, but by design.
>
> — Fisher, Frey, and Hattie (2016)

- ☐ **Every student**—not just some students, such as those whose parents can afford it or those who are lucky enough to live on a street that allows them to attend an amazing school.
- ☐ **Deserves**—yes, we believe that students have the right to a quality education.
- ☐ **A great teacher**—one who develops strong relationships, employs culturally fortifying practices, knows his or her content and how to teach it, and evaluates his or her impact.
- ☐ **Not by chance**—meaning that we have to move beyond the luck of the draw that permeates much of the educational landscape.
- ☐ **But by design**—yes, there are learning designs that work, when used at the right time.

Summary

Culturally fortified learning environments have a sustaining influence on how members of the collective show up. They move us from isolation to cooperation, from only seeing windows to experiencing mirrors, from product driven to purpose driven, from individualism to collectivism, and from self-preservation to self-regulation. These environments dismantle the hidden practices that squelch the human spirit. Our brains are designed for connections, community, and cognitive engagement.

These are strengthened when there is an intentional cultural cultivation. Members are able to show up and present themselves in the fullness of who they are. Cultural fortification is not a practice; it is what informs our practice as we make better decisions for eliciting, engaging, motivating, strengthening, and preserving the intellectual and individual capacity of all of our learners (Jackson, 2015).

Chapter Highlights

- In culturally fortifying environments, there is a reciprocity to strengthening all members in the learning community.

- There is a mutual responsibility to create a culture that provides an opportunity for everyone to thrive and be recognized for who they are and what they bring to the collective.

- When there is fortification, there is strength in the levels of engagement (behavioral, cognitive, and emotional).

- In fortification, we must consider how each member of the learning community is strengthened through their dimensions of identity.

- A culturally fortified learning environment requires the members of the organization to routinely display equity moves that are immediate, accessible and relatable.

- The learning community is positively impacted when there is an intentional equity focus on culturally fortifying practices in the organization.

- Culturally fortifying curriculum ensures that all students, regardless of their dimensions of identity, have an opportunity to learn, have access to rigorous academic experiences, find relevance, and make connections in the content and materials.

- When creating culturally fortifying learning environments, instructional practices are the heartbeat of students showing up ready, empowered, and motivated to learn.

- Culturally fortifying programmatic practices give life to the organization and are instrumental to all aspects of the collective.

- As we design culturally fortified learning environments, we place the student at the heart of creating collective equity.

Invitation to Collective Thinking

- How can the learning community leverage culturally fortifying practices to strengthen the individual members of the collective?

- How are the four culturally fortifying practices (organizational, curricular, programmatic, and instructional) currently aligned to your shared mission, vision, beliefs, and purpose statements?

- How will you leverage the culturally fortifying practices in your current instructional framework? Are there gaps in knowing and doing? What additional professional development is needed?

- What are some actions you can take as a learning community to sustain these practices in your organization or school?

Reflection

The Cultural Consciousness Matrix below outlines the levels of knowing that empower a collective to bridge the knowing-doing gap.

THE CULTURAL CONSCIOUSNESS MATRIX	
Level 2	**Level 3**
Consciously Unskilled	Consciously Skilled
• You know that you don't know	• You know that you have the skill
• Beginning of growth	• Comfortable with being uncomfortable
• Crisis of consciousness	• Focused confidence
• Enlightened	• Intentional
Being	**Becoming**
Level 1	**Level 4**
Unconsciously Unskilled	Unconsciously Skilled
• You don't know what you don't know	• You know the skill and the skill is second nature
• Complete lack of knowledge and skills	• Completely confident
• Fixed mindset	• Automaticity, accountability, humility
• Oblivious	• Graceful
Existing	**Evolving**

Source: Adapted from Burch (1970).

In what ways has the information in Chapter 4 closed your knowing-doing gap?

_____

_____

_____

_____

What is your knowing-doing gap?

_____

_____

_____

_____

So what does this mean for you?

_____

_____

_____

_____

Now what are your immediate actions?

_____

_____

_____

_____

Equity Dispositions for the Collective

5

Strengthening the Impact We Make on the Learning Community by Leveraging the Ways of Being

Leading for equity is about the choices you make to be aware; acknowledge the inequity you see, the dissonance you feel, and make the decision to provide support anyway.

—LaShawn Routé Chatmon, Executive Director, National Equity Project

By now, you have a sense of what it means to engage with others with a shared purpose, accountability, mutual voice, and respect when transforming environments into equitable spaces. When we embrace the conviction that equity is a way of being, we are compelled to continuously examine and reflect on how we contribute to and perpetuate inequitable practices throughout our system. To help the collective develop the skills and will to examine the impact of racial inequities and other marginalizations, we must acknowledge personal biases and fears (Harris, 2010). When we mitigate inequities and marginalizations in the learning community, we evolve in our dispositions as individuals and as a collective.

Dispositions are "the values, commitments, and professional ethics that influence behaviors toward students, families, colleagues, and communities that affect student learning, motivation, and development as well as the educator's own professional growth" (National Council for Accreditation of Teacher Education, 2002, p. 53). Our dispositions influence the manner in which we confront systems of inequity. A disposition might not be immediately visible, but it will manifest over time. Dispositions can negatively or positively impact the progress of the collective. Negative dispositions will impede the commitment to transform environments into equitable learning spaces. Positive dispositions help teachers respond in professionally appropriate ways and be aware of how their own cultural background may predispose their views and actions (Carroll, 2007; Thornton, 2006).

It is our deep belief that when we evolve, others evolve. Systems evolve, organizations evolve, and communities evolve. In school districts and learning communities across the nation, we have experienced the evolution of educators who have committed to unlearning, updating, refining, and reconsidering the ways in which they promote collective equity. This evolution is furthered by collective equity professional learning, executive equity coaching, and equitable transformation coaching. This brings joy and excitement as we witness the movement of learning communities on the journey toward transforming their environments into equitable learning spaces.

 Jot Thought

Reflecting on Personal Dispositions for Equity

Using the Reflecting on Personal Dispositions for Equity Assessment below, identify where you are with your personal dispositions. Once completed, discuss the implications for your collective equity journey with your equity commitment partner.

PERSONAL DISPOSITIONS FOR EQUITY	FREQUENCY OF ACTIONS			
	NEVER	RARELY	SOMETIMES	OFTEN
1. I use language that promotes belief in the abilities of all members in the learning community.				
2. I acknowledge my own biased behaviors that are apparent in my thoughts, language, and actions.				
3. I encourage risk taking and create brave spaces for open dialogue about race and hard conversations regarding existing inequities in our learning communities.				
4. I possess the capacity and stamina to consciously feel discomfort while increasing my cultural understanding about other dimensions of identity and racial inequities.				
5. I am motivated to seek diverse perspectives in order to refine and reconsider my mental models and implicit biases about others.				
6. I believe in the capability of others to collectively disrupt educational disparities.				

PERSONAL DISPOSITIONS FOR EQUITY	FREQUENCY OF ACTIONS			
	NEVER	RARELY	SOMETIMES	OFTEN
7. I actively join movements that don't personally impact me.				
8. I create opportunities to engage my students and families on identified topics of interest and needs within their community.				
9. I believe that my contributions, voice, and specific actions create opportunities for others to learn from and with me as an equity partner.				
10. I stay the course when I experience equity fatigue because of the urgency for others to heal, experience shared power, and show up in the fullness of who they are.				

 Available for download from resources.corwin.com/CollectiveEquity

Cultural Sustainability

When we come together and form the collective, we intentionally build trust, immediacy, intimacy, belonging, and efficacy. These collective actions give birth to the positive dispositions of members of the learning community. When collectives build personal connections, strengthen their interconnectedness, and honor dimensions of identity, the doorways are opened for sharing our lived experiences. As we share our lived experiences, we commit to valuing diversity and culture other than our own. When we cultivate this type of environment within the learning community, we establish cultural sustainability. Cultural sustainability is a commitment to preserving the cultures, languages, and full identities of the individuals who make up our learning community. It is the impetus to maintaining a living, breathing, and fortifying environment that is strengthened by the diversity of the collective.

How does the collective cultivate cultural sustainability? This fundamental question often engages educators at the surface level of culture, resulting in actions that have a low emotional impact on trust. As an example, schoolwide celebrations such as international festivals where the focus is on food, dances, clothing, hairstyles, and other external cultural representations fail to address the deep levels of culture. In order to fully answer our question, educators have to consider all levels of culture, examine organizational practices, disrupt biased beliefs, and identify ways to deepen equitable practices to validate all members of the learning community. Cultural validation can create socially and emotionally trusting environments. As we discussed in Chapter 3, trust is essential if an organization is to succeed—both in beliefs and action. Trust is the nexus of forming deep sustaining relationships that are interdependent. Cultural sustainability empowers the members of the learning community intellectually, socially, and emotionally.

✎ Jot Thought

Cultivating Cultural Sustainability

Critical questions to ask in cultivating cultural sustainability:

Are we authentic in what we are doing and are we holding each other accountable?

_____

_____

_____

Do our actions reflect our beliefs?

_____

_____

_____

Are you engaging in intentional conversations and actions that result in the acceleration of fortifying relationships? If so, to what degree?

_____

_____

_____

What are your specific actions as a collective to sustain cultural connections?

_____

_____

_____

_____

_____

From Systems to Classrooms

There is a funnel effect that occurs when moving from cultivating the cultural sustainability of the collective to implementing culturally relevant pedagogy in our instructional practice. When the collective of professionals affirms the intersecting identities of the individuals who form the collective, this strengths-based orientation filters down to our instructional practices, including the relationships we form with our students and their families. Engaging in courageous conversations holds us accountable to the actions that affirm, strengthen, and sustain those who we serve. This matters because all members of the learning community win as a result of how we value and respond to the diverse dimensions of identity. Culturally sustaining environments enhance all voices and shared values as well as promoting agency and efficacy.

 Collective Equity Voices

Director of Equity, Outreach, and Engagement Isaiah Johnson's Journey to Collective Equity

Isaiah Johnson started his equity journey in the Auburn School District in 2004 as the first Black assistant principal in the district. He came to the district because he noticed the changing student demographics in this area. Isaiah saw an opportunity to prepare the district for the upcoming needs of the changing school demographics. Isaiah implemented professional development focusing on culturally responsive practices for teaching and leading. In 2008, he became the first Black principal in the Auburn School District, where his impact was needed more than ever due to the school's rapid shift from being predominantly white to being a multicultural community.

In Principal Johnson's early years, he noticed disproportionalities in discipline and attendance among students of color. Other data sources revealed that students did not feel safe, connected, or that they belonged. Principal Johnson and the building leadership team shared the data with the staff and focused their attention on building relationships within the learning community. It was a desire to earn the trust of the students and their families while simultaneously strengthening relationships with every member of the student body.

Cascade Middle School adopted its mission statement—Spartan Excellence: Everyone, Everywhere, Every Day—with the intention

(Continued)

(Continued)

to create a schoolwide culture and environment where all students were fortified. They initially analyzed attendance and discipline data quarterly to monitor and ensure progress. Observations revealed that those intervals were not enough. Although there was improvement, they wanted to do more. Principal Johnson and the leadership team challenged staff to do a "Focus 5" strategy. This strategy required all staff to select five of their most challenging students and create intentional meeting opportunities that were non-instructional. It was no surprise that most of the challenging students were students of color. Through the implementation of this strategy, they noticed staff being more proactive when addressing challenging behaviors, and the impact on students resulted in higher levels of respect and authentic relationships with the adult members in the school. This awareness and intentionality created a school environment that supported students academically, socially, and emotionally. Cascade Middle experienced a positive shift in the attendance and discipline data for all students.

In addition to the Focus 5 strategy, the school leadership team implemented the Deep Equity Framework to continue to deepen their relationships with students and incorporate Gary Howard's (2014) seven principles for culturally responsive teaching. Also, staff engaged in uncomfortable conversations around race, socioeconomics, and other dimensions of difference. Principal Johnson recalled one of his staff members sharing how they "did not see color." Through staff discussions, the team was able to recognize how being "color blind" was not culturally responsive and negated who students were. Cascade Middle School was able to create a welcoming culture where students felt valued, seen, safe, cared for, and understood. The leadership team developed activities for the staff and students to share their cultural stories and lived experiences so fortification, appreciation, and respect could be experienced by all in the learning community.

Once Principal Johnson and the leadership team established this practice as a part of their culture, another culturally responsive teaching principle was added every year. Principal Johnson was proud to say that in the number of students being removed from the classroom decreased and more teacher-student relationships developed. This continued until Isaiah's departure to his role as Director of Equity, Family Engagement, and Outreach. He worked to include equity into leadership at all levels. Director Johnson is motivated to add culturally responsive practices to all districtwide initiatives, with a strong focus on youth equity stewardship.

Realizing collective equity in action:
How did Principal Johnson's focus on the implementation of culturally responsive teaching practices sustain the members of the learning community?

- Who benefitted?

- In what ways did they benefit?

- What was the degree of the benefit?

- What connections can you make to Principal Johnson's journey to realizing collective equity in action?

_____

_____

_____

_____

Collective Efficacy

How does our relationship to our collective influence our effectiveness as culturally relevant practitioners? Recall from Chapter 4 that culturally fortified learning environments move us from isolation to cooperation, from only seeing windows to experiencing mirrors, from product driven to purpose driven, from individualism to collectivism, and from self-regulation to self-actualization. By being open to and honoring the diverse backgrounds, life experiences, and identities of the adults in the collective, we gain a better appreciation of those differences in our student population(s), and consequently our ability to succeed as a practitioner is augmented.

Yet even with the best intentions, sometimes teams experience limited to no success in transforming their learning community. When faced with evidence of limited or no impact, we lose our motivation to see our well-crafted plans to the end. The hard truth is that, in the absence of tangible evidence of improvement, we become demoralized, we lose momentum, and our work is hijacked. However, some teams are able to face these challenges and overcome inertia. Typically, these are teams with a high sense of *collective efficacy.*

In order to have collective efficacy across a community, we must first have self-efficacy as individuals. "Self-efficacy is a personal judgement about how well one can execute courses of action required to deal with perspective situations" (Bandura, 1982, p. 122). When we truly believe our actions lead us closer to meeting our goals, we move closer to collective efficacy. "Collective teacher efficacy refers to a staff's shared belief that through their collective actions, they can positively influence student outcomes, including for students who are disengaged and/or disadvantaged" (Fisher, Frey, & Smith, 2020, p. 4). Learning communities with high teacher collective efficacy demonstrate the following characteristics: optimism that all students will learn, confidence in their abilities to reach and teach all students, and the stamina to be committed to success (Bloomberg & Pitchford, 2016).

However, for teams to experience sustained impact in equitable learning environments, collective teacher efficacy alone will not get the job done. There must be an interaction between credibility and teacher collective efficacy. Credibility in organizations is present when the adults are believable, convincing, and capable of persuading all members that they can be successful in the learning community (Fisher et al., 2020). And to go even further, credibility in transformative equitable learning environments is fostered through a combination of trustworthiness, honesty, competence, and commitment as perceived by members of the learning community. Credibility with an equity lens requires the realization and validation of the prior historical experiences of the learning community, especially in communities serving BIPOC. When members of the collective demonstrate efficacy and credibility with a laser-like focus on equity, their ability to mitigate patterns of disparity and oppression of voice, value, and agency increases exponentially.

Figure 5.1 identifies seven collective actions that elevate a commitment to sustain equitable ways of being. It is important to note that these collective actions may not occur in a linear fashion.

FIGURE 5.1   Collective Actions That Bring Value to Transformative Equitable Learning Environments

In transformative equitable learning environments, the collective engages in the following:

1. We analyze our impact on disrupting inequitable practices.

2. We learn culturally relevant pedagogy from and with each other.

3. We engage in difficult conversations around race, class, sexual orientations, and other intersecting identities.

4. We investigate and expose our biases.

5. We reflect on our roles as culturally fortifying educators.

6. We continue on the journey toward diminishing systems of inequity.

7. We demonstrate cultural humility in a world of multifaceted expectations to disrupt systems of oppression.

 Shared Experience

Collective Actions That Bring Value to Transformative Equitable Learning Environments

1. **We analyze our impact on disrupting inequitable practices.**

Analyzing our impact means that we are continuously and consistently monitoring and assessing our actions (see the collective engagement by design process in Chapter 2). The collective must be reflective and responsive to the needs of all learning community members, providing an opportunity to move from the "autopsy model," in which educators bypass opportunities to examine root causes of educational disparities (Reeves, 2006), to immediate actions and attention.

Shared Truths:

    a. Can your learning community identify its current reality by analyzing data?

    b. Do the members know their individual and collective impact?

    c. Is there a process to identify "who is benefiting and who is not?" (Fisher et al., 2019)

(Continued)

(Continued)

2. **We learn culturally relevant pedagogy from and with each other.**

The community agreements discussed in Chapter 1 form the foundation of how we work, share experiences, and come together to create brave and inclusive spaces. We share a laser-like focus on diminishing the negative experiences and outcomes for all too many in the learning community through the ways in which we engage. We create opportunities to honor, value, and respect the knowledge, perspective, and voices of the collective.

Shared Truths:

a. In what ways does your collective come together to share knowledge using the Collective Equity Framework (see Chapter 1)?

b. What structures and practices are in place to enable all members to learn from and with each other to identify and diminish the negative experiences of students, staff, and parents?

3. **We engage in difficult conversations around race, class, sexual orientations, and other intersecting identities.**

These conversations are grounded in our awareness that all members of our collective embody personal and cultural identities as well as lived experiences that shape their interactions and responses to oppressive policies and practices, inequity, and social justice. In response to the discomfort that frequently surfaces in such conversations, we strive to become unconsciously skilled, as identified in the Cultural Consciousness Matrix (see Chapter 1), in relentlessly challenging the imbalances of power and privilege that impact our organizations.

Shared Truths:

a. In what ways do all members add their voices to the conversations about oppressive structures, policies, and practices that influence the learning community?

b. Are the members using the Cultural Consciousness Matrix to journey through the levels of knowing in order to evolve toward collective equity?

   c. What are the fears that impede the learning community from engaging in these difficult conversations? How will you overcome those fears as a collective?

4. **We investigate and expose our biases.**

Increasing self-awareness, especially honing our understanding of how our thoughts impact our actions, is an integral part of our work. Eliminating unconscious and conscious biases, stereotypes, and prejudices that stifle the growth of the learning community is an integral part of our transformation into equitable fortifying environments.

Shared Truths:

   a. Who are you in relation to the collective? How do your beliefs impact your actions? Are your beliefs fortifying the learning community and in what ways?

   b. What are the barriers and biases that your collective perpetuates that hinder the growth of the learning community?

   c. How will you examine and eliminate the barriers that hinder the growth of the learning community?

5. **We reflect on our roles as culturally fortifying educators.**

First we ask ourselves, Who is being fortified and who is not and to what degree? When we have the will to learn about other's cultural experiences, backgrounds, and dimensions of identity, we demonstrate cultural humility, a concept introduced in Chapter 1. We strive to become more comfortable with our discomfort and push ourselves to take immediate actions that are necessary for growth and progress in creating transformative equitable learning environments.

Shared Truths:

   a. What fortifying structures, processes, and practices are being implemented for all members in your learning community? (Refer to Chapter 4)

   b. What data will help you monitor and assess the impact of fortifying learning environments?

   c. As a collective, what are your action plans for fortifying all members in the learning community?

(Continued)

(Continued)

6. **We continue on the journey toward diminishing systems of inequity.**

We accept that there is no "end point" to this work. Rather, we acknowledge that it is an ongoing journey and we never fully "arrive" at cultural competency. When we accept this lack of closure, we are better equipped to diminish systems of inequity and structures that devalue individual and collective identities. It is humbling to acknowledge that we are never fully "woke," but, at the same time, it fuels our commitment to continue the learning journey and our hunger for equity for all. The collective bravely addresses oppressive structures and issues that continue to plague the hearts, minds, and spirits of the members of the learning community. On this journey we identify equity pathways, the roadmaps to equitable transformations, and equity pavers, the steps to acquire the requisite knowledge, attitudes, and skills that guide us along our equity pathway.

Shared Truths:

    a. What is (are) your equity pathway(s)?

    b. What are your hopes and dreams for diminishing systems of inequity?

    c. What immediate equity pavers are necessary for cultural humility?

7. **We demonstrate cultural humility in a world of multifaceted expectations to disrupt systems of oppression.**

When we *sustain* the inner and outer (and never-ending) work of transforming equitable learning environments, we better our odds of disrupting systems of oppression. Cultural humility is an equitable, proactive disposition that is "a lifelong process of self-reflection and self-critique whereby the individual not only learns about another's culture, but starts with an examination of her/his own beliefs and cultural identities" (Tervalon & Murray-Garcia, 1998). This disposition addresses the power imbalances that hinder the reciprocity of relationships, erode trust, and impact how individuals engage and interact in the collective. Power hoarding has no place in the collective!

Shared Truths:

    a. What are the multifaceted expectations you are addressing to diminish systems of inequity in your learning community?

b.   What has been the inner and outer work of your collective?

c.   What is harming the work of your collective?

d.   What is your collective's plan for acquiring cultural humility?

 Jot Thought

Bring Value to Transformative Equitable Learning Environments

How are you engaging with your collective at the relational, professional, organizational, and systemic levels to create transformative equitable learning environments? What actions are you taking to address systems of inequity in your learning community?

THE COLLECTIVE EQUITY FRAMEWORK ELEMENTS	YOUR ENGAGEMENT	RESULTS/NEXT ACTIONS
Personal (You)		
Relational (You and a colleague)		
Professional (You and your grade level)		
Organizational (You and your school)		
Systemic (You and your community)		

 Available for download from resources.corwin.com/CollectiveEquity

Collective Equity Dispositions

If we lived in this world alone, we would have no need to evolve into social beings. The simple fact is that we need one another. We need to acknowledge that we are interdependent and interconnected with the human race. Our inner spirits are strengthened when we come together through common values, beliefs, aspirations, and interests to form reciprocal relationships. Our ways of being and nurturing each other's spirits in our learning community are reinforced by our collective equity dispositions.

Collective equity dispositions are a major component of equitable learning environments. Our collective equity dispositions influence our decisions and the manner in which we choose (consciously or unconsciously) to interrogate (or not interrogate) systems of inequity. Figure 5.2 lists 10 collective equity dispositions that we should strive to embody in the interest of strengthening our impact as individuals and as a collective.

FIGURE 5.2   Collective Equity Dispositions

1. Cultural humility: A lifelong commitment equity

2. Cultural humility + Versatility: An ability to forgo individual perspectives for the good of collective equity

3. Cultural humility + Agency: An ability to act on one's own behalf to design transformative equitable learning environments

4. Cultural humility + Efficacy: An ability to believe in and act upon one's capability to organize and execute collective equity

5. Cultural humility + Agility: An ability to proactively respond without being derailed when addressing structural inequities

6. Cultural humility + Reflexivity: An ability to have the courage to examine biased beliefs and assumptions

7. Cultural humility + Solidarity: An ability to strengthen group cohesion and foster a sense of belonging among the members of the collective

8. Cultural humility + Vulnerability: An ability to take risks by sharing one's feelings, flaws, and uncertainties and be comfortable with being uncomfortable

9. Cultural humility + Collectivity: An ability to be accountable to more than just oneself to achieve educational equity for all

10. Cultural humility + Mutuality: An ability to depend on each other to cultivate environments that are equitable and fortifying to all

---

Cultural Humility

Cultural humility is the mother of all collective equity dispositions. It is a proactive disposition that is the foundation for designing transformative equitable learning environments. Cultural humility is defined as "a lifelong process of self-reflection and self-critique" that starts with an examination of one's own beliefs and culture (Tervalon & Murray-Garcia, 1998). When we commit to cultural humility, we embark on a journey to self-awareness and grace where we relentlessly challenge the imbalances of power and privilege that impact the way in which we see ourselves, others, and the world around us.

When the collective operates with cultural humility, there is perpetual grappling with the following:

- What do we need to unlearn? (e.g., biased beliefs, closed-minded perspectives, and mental models of individuals and their cultural representation)

- What do we need to update? (e.g., views on the world around us, levels of culture, models of instruction, cultural relevance)

- What do we need to refine? (e.g., professional practice, how we forge relationships, our personal commitment to our moral imperative for educating all)

- What do we need to reconsider? (e.g., our beliefs about others, our motivation for equity work, what it will take to create transformative equitable learning environments)

Cultural humility drives us to move beyond the Golden Rule to the Platinum Rule: We treat others how they want, expect, and deserve to be treated.

Versatility

Versatility is the capacity to read and respond to our environment, particularly the current inequities and their impact on the learning community. Versatility is grounded in self-knowledge but, at the same time, it gives us the ability to honor and accept the perspectives of others. Versatility enables us to consciously step into unfamiliar and uncomfortable spaces that broaden our understanding and appreciation of others' cultural affiliations, lived experiences, and dimensions of identity. With a versatile disposition, we are able and willing to forgo our individual perspectives and comfort for the good of creating collective equity.

Disrupting Inequities

Versatility disrupts the collective stagnation and the intentional unwillingness to promote culturally fortifying practices.

Agency

Agency is the capacity to act on our own behalf, fueled by the belief in our ability to effect change. Building the agency of the collective requires investing in the professional capital of the group (Hargreaves & Fullan, 2012). It calls for the collective to tap into its intrinsic motivation and create a sense of urgency for cultivating the requisite knowledge, attitudes, and skills to design transformative equitable learning environments. Our collective agency is influenced by shared visions, ongoing collaborations, implementation of fortifying practices, monitoring and providing feedback, and taking the time to recognize and celebrate small wins toward equitable transformations.

Disrupting Inequities

Agency disrupts the inner voice of doubt. When we have agency, we have the capability to disrupt the experiences of those that have been historically disenfranchised and oppressed. Having agency gives us pride in the ability to shape the trajectory of life experiences for all members of the collective.

Efficacy

Efficacy is the belief in one's capabilities to organize and execute a course of action. When we believe in our ability to succeed in a particular situation, our odds of actual success increase. Efficacy encompasses our thinking, behavior, and emotions (Bandura, 1977). Efficacy grounds us in a determination to pursue success in the midst of challenging conditions. The disposition of efficacy enables us to recover from disappointments, feelings of failure, and setbacks because we look at adversity as a challenge rather than a threat. This sense of optimism and confidence provides intrinsic motivation to stay the course.

Disrupting Inequities

Efficacy disrupts crises of confidence. It is the belief that we can have an impact on dismantling the systems of inequity in the learning community. When we have efficacy, we are relentless in staying the course in our mission to create transformative, equitable learning environments.

Agility

Agility is the ability to proactively respond without being derailed by the flavors of the week, dueling initiatives, or political log jams that prevent momentum. A culture that embraces the disposition of agility is a culture that nurtures trust and empowers learners to navigate barriers with skill and grace. When the collective embodies the disposition of agility, there is a consistent improvement in how we fortify the learning community. Agile cultures tinker with the equity pathways to identify equity pavers that work best to design transformative equitable learning environments.

Disrupting of Inequities

Agility disrupts the inability to focus and the desire to jump on trendy equity "bandwagons" that lack substance, direction, vision, and sustained practices. When the collective is agile, our desire to find a quick fix is replaced by the courage to take the time to truly transform our learning environments into places in which we can belong.

Reflexivity

Reflexivity is the capacity for self-reflection. In the context of transformative equity work, we have the courage to examine our social and cultural biases, assumptions, judgements, and motives and to understand how such "baggage" can shape and influence the manner in which we manage the dynamics of difference. According to Bolton and Delderfield (2018), reflexivity enables inquiry through an examination of personal experience and exploration of the values and viewpoints that underpin behaviors. Reflexivity leads to reciprocity and increases relational trust. With the disposition of reflexivity, we observe, examine, and challenge the inconsistencies and inequities in the learning community.

Disrupting Inequities

Reflexivity disrupts the one-sided viewpoints and perspectives birthed out of personal experiences, individualistic stances, assumptions, and cultural affiliations that impede collective equity. When we move beyond reflection to reflexivity, then we are able to design transformative equitable learning environments.

Solidarity

Activist and Black Panther co-founder Bobby Seale once stated, "You don't fight racism with racism. The best way to fight racism is with solidarity." In other words, it is ill-advised to go into battle alone; we are stronger when we act in solidarity with one another. Solidarity is a sense of fellowship displayed by members of a collective who are united by shared purposes, responsibilities, and interests. The disposition of solidarity strengthens group cohesion and fosters a sense of belonging that strengthens the commitment of a group of individuals to one another. Solidarity is the impetus for relational trust and respect. The trust and respect that often flow from solidarity and collective identities can enable individuals to work together in response to shifting socioecological conditions (Pretty & Ward, 2001; Adger, 2003). Solidarity fuels our collective sense of urgency to sustain our actions aimed at disturbing the structures, systems, and practices that perpetuate inequities.

Disrupting Inequities

Solidarity disrupts the belief that equity work can be done in silos. This disposition enables the collective to leverage their diverse skills and knowledge to disturb inequitable practices in the learning community.

Vulnerability

"Vulnerability is the birthplace of love, belonging, joy, courage, empathy, and creativity" (Brown, 2012). This disposition enables you to face who you are and what changes you would like to see in your life and the world around you. You take risks by sharing your feelings, flaws, and uncertainties and are comfortable with being uncomfortable. When we take risks, embrace our vulnerabilities, and expose current truths, the members of the learning community experience stronger connections. The disposition of vulnerability is the bedrock of cultural humility.

Disrupting Inequities

The disposition of vulnerability disrupts the fear of being exposed and is typically taboo in individualistic cultures. Vulnerability gives us the courage to journey toward cultural humility.

Collectivity

The disposition of collectivity is foundational for groups to establish shared truths, relational interdependence, and common ambitions. When there is collectivity, the group prioritizes the common good of all members. Collectivity is an act of giving to others, and in transformative equitable learning environments, it translates to a belief that by working together and being accountable to more than just oneself, we can achieve educational equity for all.

Disrupting Inequities

The disposition of collectivity provides an antidote to current systems grounded in principles of individualism and competition. Collectivity replaces deeply engrained competitive values and behaviors with the group's commitment to common ambitions, a willingness to embrace inclusivity, and designing spaces of collective equity.

Mutuality

The disposition of mutuality is the ability to depend on each other to cultivate environments that are equitable and fortifying for all. It requires a willingness to come together in respect, trust, and compromise. There is a level of dependency that bolsters the relationship. In order to bring this disposition of mutuality to life, collaboration, cooperation, and relational trust are paramount.

Disrupting Inequities

The disposition of mutuality rejects siloed behaviors and individualistic mindsets. The support for one another mitigates equity fatigue and feelings of despair. Mutuality unsettles biased beliefs and esteems the commitment to each other's journey toward creating transformative equitable learning environments.

 Shared Experience

How do members of your learning community commit to embodying the collective equity dispositions in order to disrupt inequities?

Engagement Task: Record yourself on video displaying each disposition, for the purpose of self-reflection and peer feedback. Write your answers to the following questions in the table that follows.

Self-Reflection

a. What do you see or hear that confirms your assumptions regarding your ability to display this disposition?

(Continued)

(Continued)

b.   What may be a stumbling block to the display of this disposition?

c.   What do you want to be sure to do again?

Peer Feedback

a.   When reviewing the Engagement Task, did you see the identified disposition?

b.   What was the impact on the learning community?

c.   What should be replicated?

DISPOSITIONS	SELF-REFLECTION	PEER FEEDBACK
Cultural Humility		
Versatility		
Agency		
Efficacy		
Agility		
Reflexivity		
Solidarity		
Vulnerability		
Collectivity		
Mutuality		

Summary

The primary focus of this chapter is on the dispositions that fuel the work of the collective in our quest to design culturally sustaining learning communities. We introduced the concept of culturally relevant pedagogy and its application to instructional level practice and association with cultural sustainability. We also unpacked the meaning of collective efficacy in the context of equity work, i.e., the belief in our collective ability to disrupt systems of oppression in our schools and beyond. This discussion culminated in a list of collective actions that we commit to in order to further our goals. Finally, we identified a set of 10 core dispositions that we strive to embody in the interest of strengthening our impact as individuals and as a collective.

Chapter Highlights

- Cultural sustainability is a commitment to preserving the cultures, languages, and full identities of the individuals who make up our learning community. It is the impetus to maintaining a living, breathing, and fortifying environment that is strengthened by the diversity of the collective.

- How does the collective cultivate cultural sustainability? Trust is essential if an organization is to succeed—both in beliefs and action. Trust is the nexus of forming deep sustaining relationships that are interdependent.

- Our shared belief in the importance of cultural sustainability filters down to our instructional pedagogy. Engaging in these courageous conversations holds us accountable to the relevant actions that strengthen and affirm the students and families we serve.

- In the absence of tangible evidence of improvement, we become demoralized, we lose momentum, and our work is hijacked. However, some teams are able to face these challenges and overcome inertia. Typically, these are teams with a high sense of collective efficacy.

- The gateway to collective efficacy is self-efficacy. "Self-efficacy is a personal judgement about how well one can execute courses of action required to deal with prospective situations" (Bandura, 1982, pp. 122). Collective efficacy refers to a staff's shared belief that through their collective actions, they can positively influence student outcomes.

- There must be an interaction between credibility and teacher collective efficacy. Credibility in transformative equitable learning environments is present when the adults are believable, convincing, and capable, as perceived by members of the learning community.

- Dispositions shape behaviors and interactions among the members in the organization and are guided by our beliefs and attitudes related to our values.

- Collective equity dispositions are a major ingredient of equitable learning environments.

- Cultural humility is a proactive equitable disposition that is foundational for all the members of the collective. It is the mother of all collective equity dispositions.

Invitation to Collective Thinking

- Discuss some actions your learning community will take to build connections in order to strengthen interconnectedness and honor dimensions of identity.

- Ladson-Billings (1995) argues that culturally relevant pedagogy does more than "fit" school culture to student culture; it also seeks to "use" student culture as a basis for classroom practice and enhance and affirm cultural competence, academic development, and social and political awareness. What are some intentional actions that learning communities can take to create culturally relevant pedagogy?

- How will members of your learning community promote teacher collective efficacy and credibility when addressing inequitable practices identified in the organization?

- Select three collective equity dispositions for your collective to implement with consistency over the next six weeks. Set aside time weekly to discuss the success of the implementation of these dispositions, calling out disruption to inequitable practices based upon their implementation.

Reflection

The Cultural Consciousness Matrix outlines the levels of knowing that empower a collective to bridge the knowing-doing gap.

THE CULTURAL CONSCIOUSNESS MATRIX	
Level 2	Level 3
Consciously Unskilled	Consciously Skilled
• You know that you don't know	• You know that you have the skill
• Beginning of growth	• Comfortable with being uncomfortable
• Crisis of consciousness	• Focused confidence
• Enlightened	• Intentional
Being	**Becoming**
Level 1	Level 4
Unconsciously Unskilled	Unconsciously Skilled
• You don't know what you don't know	• You know the skill and the skill is second nature
• Complete lack of knowledge and skills	• Completely confident
• Fixed mindset	• Automaticity, accountability, humility
• Oblivious	• Graceful
Existing	**Evolving**

Source: Adapted from Burch (1970).

In what ways has the information in Chapter 5 closed your knowing-doing gap?

_____

_____

_____

_____

What is your knowing-doing gap?

_____

_____

_____

_____

So what does this mean for you?

_____

_____

_____

_____

Now what are your immediate actions?

_____

_____

_____

_____

Realizing the Promise of Collective Equity

6

Designing Transformative Equitable Learning Environments

//

> *Not everything that is faced can be changed, but nothing can be changed until it is faced.*
>
> **—James Baldwin**

Collective equity calls out all members of the learning community to play an active role in transforming the system. As individuals and as a collective, we commit to disrupting systems of oppression and inequity in the learning community. Part of this process is becoming conscious of where we are, our desired destination, and our design for how we will get there. In previous chapters, we identified the components of our equity "GPS": equity pathways and equity pavers. Later in this chapter, we will unpack these concepts in greater detail.

To gain momentum when designing transformative equitable learning environments, we tap into our lens of consciousness, identify the appropriate resources, develop the structures for difficult conversations, implement culturally fortifying practices, and create learning partnerships with internal and external equity champions. Recognizing and confronting educational disparities that persist in our schools demands honesty, strength, perseverance, and resilience to stay the course. It is so much easier to give up, but can we? This is a question that collective organizations must continuously ask in order to devote themselves to the promise of collective equity.

Leading for Collective Equity

"A leader for equity and excellence understands that the most important issue in public education is creating schools that are both equitable and excellent" (Scheurich & Skrla, 2003, p. 100). A **collective equity leader** masters the attributes of relational leadership to design transformative equitable learning environments. These attributes are built on one's personal skills and inner abilities, all of which can be developed. Leadership attributes are strengthened by values, integrity, dispositions, motivations, habits, traits, style and behaviors.

Leading for equity requires a display of the following leadership attributes:

- Authenticity

- Inclusivity

- Humility

- Relatability

Relational leadership acknowledges the variability of time and place and the need for leaders to mold their leadership to the situation (Eacott, 2018). With these attributes, the collective equity leader takes action to empower and guide the members of the learning community to become culturally sustaining educators. Such leaders maintain a laser-like focus on the individual and shared needs of the collective. When leading equity work, Nicole and Sonja strive to engender these relational leadership attributes, as noted in the examples below.

Collective Equity Leadership Attributes

Authenticity

Leaders with an awareness of their strengths and limitations demonstrate a genuineness and vulnerability in the connections that they make within the community. Collective equity leaders realize that equity transformation is an endless learning journey; nevertheless, there is a relentless commitment to create learning environments that dismantle the inequities that are present in the organization. Collective equity leaders who embody authenticity engender trust and empower and inspire those around them to also display this attribute. They put the goals of the collective ahead of their own interests, and it is apparent in everything they do.

Highly attuned to their environments, authentic leaders rely on an intuition born of formative, sometimes harsh experiences to understand the expectations and concerns of the people they seek to influence. They retain their distinctiveness as individuals, yet they know how to win acceptance in strong corporate and social cultures and how to use elements of those cultures as a basis for radical change (Goffee & Jones, 2005, p. 88).

When Nicole is coaching for equity, she is aware of when to push and pull based on the stamina of members in the learning community. Nicole is real and relevant while simultaneously being direct and gentle in her ability to connect with learners on their journey toward equity. Her genuine aura is rooted in her desire to extract people's personal best. Often members display a transparency and vulnerability in stating what they don't know. As a relational leader, Nicole is able to cultivate spaces where they can be brave and passionate about where they are in their equity journey.

Inclusivity

Inclusive leaders thrive on leveraging the diversity of the learning community. They recognize and harness the talents and strengths of the collective. They lead with their heart, head, and hands, embracing individual talents and experiences, and tap our moral imperative to serve the greater good. Collective equity leaders foster a culture of voice, value, and validation while building relational trust. Through words and actions, they create safe and brave spaces for all members in the organization. They have an awareness of the conscious and unconscious biases in themselves as well as in the members of the collective.

> Diversity is about counting, but inclusion is about cultivating.
>
> —Vernā Myers (2016)

Nicole and Sonja know that equity work is for everyone. They are relentless in ensuring that learning communities are inclusive spaces for all: all engagements start with connections or check ins and discussion protocols bring all voices, shared power, and differing perspectives. As collective equity leaders, Nicole and Sonja work to foster environments where courage is a virtue, yet they acknowledge and appreciate silence and reflectivity as a way to fortify thinking and differing perspectives. Nicole and Sonja are diligent at integrating all members in the learning community regardless of their position, dimensions of identity, or fear of participating.

Humility

Humility is an appreciation of others' strengths and contributions. A humble leader celebrates the growth and progress of the collective. Collective equity leaders mitigate power imbalances, treating everyone with respect and dignity. A humble leader offers grace and accepts guidance for braving the true quest of leading the transformative process of designing equitable learning environments.

Without humility there is no fortification; without fortification, there are no collective actions. Nicole and Sonja value the quality of being humble and putting the needs of others at the forefront of learning. They think about what the members of the learning community need. They are consistent and recognize their own limitations. They realize that their humility is not a sign of meekness or powerlessness, but an inner strength that empowers them to coach and lead for equity. Nicole and Sonja's humility allows them to lead by example. As culturally humble leaders, they respect the members of the learning community and believe that those they serve are able to design transformative equitable learning communities.

> Relatable leaders know their values, know their value, know the value of others, and know how to add value to others.
>
> —Maxwell (2019)

Relatability

Being a relatable leader is being yourself in the face of difficulty. It is knowing how to be cognizant of what the collective needs in the moment that they need it. It requires listening intently, staying curious and connected, and leveraging what has been and what needs to be. The collective equity leader is not oblivious to historical inequities and systems of oppression but is dedicated to the shared vision of designing transformative equitable learning environments.

As a collective equity consultant, Sonja is aware of the diverse ways learners show up with different perspectives, lived experiences, and mental models. It is necessary for Sonja to understand how individuals enter spaces and express ways of being as they are on their equity journey while also constantly surveying the needs of all members in the learning community. Sonja works hard to honor each voice while tuning in to the back stories that often are overlooked. Being on her own equity journey enables Sonja to make deep connections. Relatability can break down the barriers that could otherwise impede the design of transformative equitable learning environments.

Jot Thought

Reflecting on Collective Equity Leadership Attributes

Using the Reflecting on Collective Equity Leadership Attributes Assessment below, identify where you are with your leadership attributes and then discuss the implications for your journey toward collective equity with your equity commitment partner.

EQUITY-FOCUSED LEADERSHIP ATTRIBUTES	FREQUENCY OF ACTIONS			
	NEVER	RARELY	SOMETIMES	OFTEN
1. I exhibit a relentless commitment to creating learning environments that disrupt systems of inequities by demonstrating my personal vulnerability and genuine passion for this work.				
2. I intentionally include others in order to expand the collective's personal and professional knowledge and skills.				
3. I appreciate the contributions of others and I continuously look for ways to elevate and enhance voices and share power within the collective.				
4. I am cognizant that relationships and my ability to cultivate them are paramount in all aspects of equity work.				
5. I intentionally empower others to improve their knowledge, skills, dispositions, stamina, and commitment to the promise of collective equity.				

 Available for download from resources.corwin.com/CollectiveEquity

 Jot Thought

Amplifying the Collective Equity Leadership Attributes

List ways to amplify each of the following collective equity leadership attributes in your learning community.

COLLECTIVE EQUITY LEADERSHIP ATTRIBUTES	HOW TO AMPLIFY THEM IN MY LEARNING COMMUNITY
Authenticity	

(Continued)

(Continued)

COLLECTIVE EQUITY LEADERSHIP ATTRIBUTES	HOW TO AMPLIFY THEM IN MY LEARNING COMMUNITY
Inclusivity	
Humility	
Relatability	

 Available for download from resources.corwin.com/CollectiveEquity

 Collective Equity Voices

Principal Stan Law's Journey to Collective Equity

One thing for certain was that the pandemic year 2020 unveiled the looming inequities for scholars at George Washington High School, the urban school that Principal Law proudly leads. The opportunity gaps that were exposed by the pandemic drove district and school officials to institute radical, comprehensive measures to ensure that all scholars could access and excel in the "new normal." At GWHS, more than 65 percent of the students receive free or reduced lunch, and more than 20 percent are English learners and students with disabilities. It is safe to say that the aforementioned groups experienced disproportionate levels of harm and "dis-ease" during the pandemic, in comparison to schools in wealthier districts. These inequities included insufficient technology (digital divide), psychological harm and trauma, and inadequate relationships with educators that compromised any sense of connectedness to the school community. Many of these inequities were present before the pandemic and demanded culturally relevant interventions.

The myriad challenges led the school community to often remind themselves of their mission: providing a rigorous and innovative curriculum in a safe and supportive environment. Such reminders kept them focused on their purpose in order to meet the needs of the most vulnerable. In response to the crisis, the central office, in collaboration with the school and business community, combined a host of resources to disrupt the inequities that left so many students even more marginalized, disenfranchised, and disconnected. As a result, the triple threat of academic, technological, and social/emotional gaps were met with services and interventions that afforded the students the opportunity to participate in learning at a consistently high level. For example, the abrupt shift to remote virtual learning required that every student have access to the Internet as well as a computer. Given the valiant efforts of the district and the school leadership team, every student in need was issued a computer and a MiFi (wireless access device) at no cost. Measures like this addressed the biggest access barrier for students being able to partake in daily, high quality instruction and connectedness to the school community.

Despite the efforts, many students still experienced disengagement, isolation, and chronic attendance issues. Undoubtedly, the COVID-19 pandemic played a factor, but even prior to the pandemic, GWHS was challenged with a high rates of chronic absenteeism, high numbers of students having to retake courses for on-track graduation, and an array of mental health and social/emotional needs experienced by students living in low-income, disadvantaged families. Disruption of what had become predictable patterns called for radical change. Hence, Principal Law scaled a highly impactful intervention that was previously limited to the senior cohort. The Student Success Agents model became full-scale for Grades 9–12 at the onset of the pandemic. This model enlisted all staff, irrespective of their role or position, including custodians, office associates, classroom assistants, graduation coaches, counselors, teachers, social workers, and other school officials, to engage students and build deep relationships that effectively addressed the full spectrum of their needs. Every student was assigned a Student Success Agent, who was responsible for weekly contacts with specific tasks for students. As a result, students were more connected, informed, and impacted by the efforts of caring adults.

Initially, this practice was not embraced by some staff members who were apprehensive about their ability to relate to students with whom they had never interacted. However, given the sense of urgency, opting out was not an option. A school mantra for GWHS was that *students come first, and all adults are responsible for the student's success*. Thus, the administrative team strategically assigned students to every staff member and took measures to cultivate their collective efficacy to ensure that they could build relational trust with their students. The average student-adult ratio was 7:1, which meant all 750 students were connected to one caring adult who would see them through the entire school year and keep in touch in successive years.

(Continued)

(Continued)

In past years, this particular culturally fortifying practice led to increased graduation rates and elevated academic success. However, given the pandemic year of 2020, GWHS students have suffered some undue academic and social hemorrhaging. Principal Law is confident that the radical measures incorporated, including Student Success Agents, will have a profoundly positive impact on student success and will greatly aid in identifying barriers and providing access to a more equitable educational experience.

Realizing collective equity in action:

What are some of the culturally fortifying practices and collective equity leadership attributes that supported Principal Stan Law in realizing collective equity?

What additional enhancements could have been implemented to realize collective equity?

_____

_____

_____

_____

Embodying these attributes isn't enough: You must also model and execute them in your daily leadership practice. We have seen leaders who value a communal stance for addressing inequities and educational disparities. They build collective efficacy; they communicate expectations; they create brave spaces; they foster relational trust; they know where they are going; they engage in difficult conversations; they develop equity partnerships; they give feedback throughout the journey; and they course correct when the learning community encounters stumbling blocks. But, most important, they cannot accomplish all this in a silo. The Collective Equity Voices example that follows highlights Indianapolis public school Principal Stan Law. His journey demonstrates leveraging the collective equity leadership attributes (inclusivity, authenticity, humility, and relatability) to support the implementation of culturally fortifying practices at George Washington High School.

Disrupting Systems of Oppression and Inequity

The interventions Principal Law and his learning community implemented to disrupt the glaring inequities at George Washington High School exemplify collective equity in action:

- Coming together

- Creating a shared vision

- Fostering relational trust

- Sustaining motivation

- Identifying fortifying practices

- Cultivating equity dispositions

- Transforming learning communities

It would be nice if we could snap our fingers and eradicate the layers of systemic and historical inequities. However, creating equitable educational opportunities for all has been an espoused goal of American educational policy since 1954 (Blackmore, 2009). Those of us who have been in this field for decades can appreciate that achieving equity will take more than new legislation (Orfield & Eaton, 1996) or carrot-and-stick accountability measures. True transformation calls for us to trouble existing systems, structures, policies, and practices of oppression and inequity.

We do this by leading, learning, and convening in ways that are inclusive of all members of the collective. Episodic spurts of professional learning and siloed initiatives aren't enough to dismantle deep-rooted systems of oppression and inequity. Siloing equity leads us to believe that equity is separate from instruction, which is separate from culture, which is separate from every other aspect of student experience and learning. However, calling out our stumbling blocks and staying focused on addressing them will point us in the direction needed to get into "good trouble."

Leading

Courageous leaders identify and call out hidden inequities or stumbling blocks that are looming in the background of even well-intentioned organizations that have engaged in the foundations of collective equity. The following are some of the more common stumbling blocks:

- Stereotype threat occurs when a person worries about doing something with which a negative perception is associated or confirms negative stereotypes about one's cultural group

- Microaggressions are statements or actions that result in indirect, subtle, or unintentional discrimination against members of marginalized cultural groups

- Equity misconceptions are instances of faulty thinking about what it means to achieve equity for all without considering systemic policies, structures, and practices that have historically oppressed different identity groups

- Supremacist views are beliefs that one group is superior to another and entitled to dominate and exclude the other

- Falsely naming barriers means not calling things what they are for the sake of protecting systemic oppressive policies, structures, and practices

- Practices not steeped in equity are superficial actions that don't address the root causes that perpetuate inequity

- Implicit bias describes our unconscious attitudes or stereotypes

- Cultural deficit theory claims that minoritized groups don't achieve in school, in life, and in society because they lack appropriate cultural values, they have shortcomings in their skills and knowledge, and they display disruptive behaviors

Learning

Begin with an equity-focused assessment of the status quo. Such an assessment reveals barriers to equity evidenced by disproportionate outcomes along racial lines, biases in our practice, and recurrent patterns of disparity. But first, we need to know where to look and what questions to ask. Common data sources that unveil disparities include the following:

- Discipline practices and patterns (e.g., disproportionate suspension rates for African American students)

- Attendance patterns

- Advanced placement criteria and referral patterns

- Disproportionality in special education referrals

- Student voice surveys and videos

- Reading Lexiles and levels

- Common formative assessments

- Achievement test scores

- Performance assessments

- Engagement rubrics

- Graduation rates

- Adult practices

- Climate surveys for all stakeholders

- Family engagement practices

Some teams limit their analysis to "big data" sources such as achievement test scores, but we can surface many hidden truths when we take the time to collect qualitative or "street data" (Safir and Dugan, 2021). Collecting street data requires us to observe, listen to, and gather artifacts from the lived experiences of stakeholders—especially those who have been marginalized. Sources include parent interviews, classroom observation data, student interviews, shadowing students, case studies, videos of teaching, feedback interviews, and home visits. These data keep us even more focused and vigilant in our quest to remove barriers to equity.

Convening

Bonded by relational trust, we convene as a collective and commit to coming together for the common good of the work of the collective. Every member of the learning community deserves educational access, rigor, relevance, and respect regardless of race, gender, ability, language, sexual orientation, family background, social class, emotional health, and all other dimensions of identity. Few would dispute that our schools couldn't function without adequate financial and human capital investment. Yet, contrary to the very meaning of equity, high-poverty schools across the United States typically receive less money than more affluent schools, both within the same district and across districts (Bireda, 2011; Equity and Excellence Commission, 2013; Hall & Ushomirsky, 2010). In the face of such blatant injustice, how can we begin to rebuild the trust that has been lost over the decades because voices have been suppressed, individuals have been invalidated, and communities have been overlooked? As individuals and as a collective, we take a stand against every system, structure, practice, and policy that perpetuates access and opportunity gaps. These gaps are perpetuated by unexamined root causes such as the following:

- Inequities in school funding

- Historic allocation of resources

- Inadequate instructional materials

- Educator expectations, particularly diminished expectations for historically marginalized groups

- Distribution of expert teachers (typically the most inexperienced teachers are assigned to the highest-need schools)

- Structural discriminatory practices (exclusionary discipline practices, BIPOC underrepresentation in gifted/talented programs and overrepresentation in special education)

In 1967, in response to widespread civil unrest, President Lyndon Johnson appointed the National Advisory Commission on Civil Disorders (also known as the Kerner Commission) to examine racial division and disparities in the United States. In 1968, the Kerner Commission issued a report concluding that the nation was "moving toward two societies, one black, one white—separate and unequal." Without major social changes, the Commission warned, the U.S. faced a "system of apartheid" in its major cities. Today, 50 years after the report was issued, that prediction characterizes most of our large urban areas, where intensifying segregation and concentrated poverty have collided with disparities in school funding to reinforce educational inequality, locking millions of students of color from low-income families out of today's knowledge-based economy. (Darling-Hammond, 2018)

> Every step toward the goal of justice requires sacrifice, suffering, and struggle; the tireless exertions and passionate concern of dedicated individuals. . . . This is no time for apathy or complacency. This is a time for vigorous and positive action.
>
> —Dr. Martin Luther King, Jr.

The words of the Kerner Commission still ring true today. In this era of national reckoning with race, we are driven by a sense of urgency as we lead, learn, and convene to sweep away the residue of historical systems of oppression and inequities that thwart our ability to serve our students and families. When we lead, learn, and convene with our heads and hearts, there is no rest for the collective until we see educational equity for all.

Engaging the Collective

The transformation process we have described requires purposeful scaffolding. We build the collective's capacity and we continuously evaluate the movement through levels of learning. In Chapter 1 we introduced you to the Cultural Consciousness Matrix, which outlines the levels of cultural consciousness that empower the collective to bridge knowing-doing gaps (see Figure 6.1). We revisited this matrix in subsequent chapters. We intentionally placed our matrix at the end of chapters to engage collectives in a process of identifying where they are, where they need to go, and equity pathways they will take to design transformative equitable environments.

FIGURE 6.1   The Cultural Consciousness Matrix

Level 2	Level 3
Consciously Unskilled	**Consciously Skilled**
• You know that you don't know	• You know that you have the skill
• Beginning of growth	• Comfortable with being uncomfortable
• Crisis of consciousness	• Focused confidence
• Enlightened	• Intentional
Being	**Becoming**
Level 1	Level 4
Unconsciously Unskilled	**Unconsciously Skilled**
• You don't know what you don't know	• You know the skill and the skill is second nature
• Complete lack of knowledge and skills	• Completely confident
• Fixed mindset	• Automaticity, accountability, humility
• Oblivious	• Graceful
Existing	**Evolving**

Source: Adapted from Burch (1970).

Equity Pathways

We introduced the concept of equity pathways in Chapter 1. A pathway, in this context, is a course of action to develop our skills, knowledge, and capacity to stay the course as we move toward equitable transformations. It organizes and leads us to specific learning experiences with a starting point, planned route, and intermediate steps to a desired destination. In coming together as the collective, we become more adept at identifying how our decisions and actions can be pathways or stumbling blocks to equity.

The goal of the Cultural Consciousness Matrix is to give the collective agency and validation that this work lives in a place of growth and human potential. As the African proverb states, *start where you are, but don't stay there.* When we openly acknowledge where we are in each quadrant of the Cultural Consciousness Matrix, we also acknowledge our desire to grow. Being transparent in addressing our gaps gives us the courage to take the necessary steps toward collective equity.

Figure 6.2, the Interracial Model of Mutual Respect developed by Bonnie Davis and Kim Anderson (2010), illustrates a four-step equity pathway:

1. Looking inside ourselves

2. Listening to and learning from others

3. Integrating new knowledge

4. A call to action

The Interracial Model of Mutual Respect gives us a process to enhance our knowledge, attitudes, skills, and dispositions—all of which are critical steps toward collective equity. The model emphasizes self-awareness, affirming our identities and those of others and learning to appreciate and better understand the lived experiences of others.

FIGURE 6.2   Interracial Model of Mutual Respect

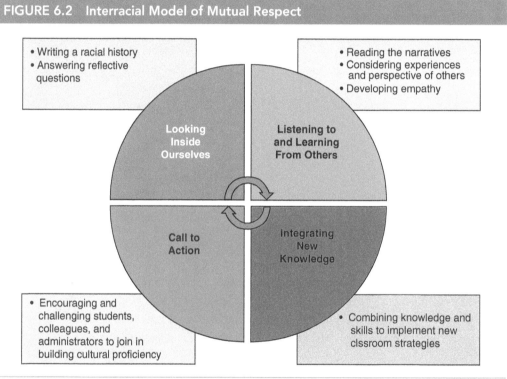

Source: Developed by Bonnie M. Davis, PhD, and Kim Anderson, MSW, LCSW, ATR-BC, ©2010. Reprinted with permission.

Equity Pavers

An equity paver is a step along our equity pathway. It is a scaffold that helps us identify the prior knowledge, attitudes, and skills of the learning community; we determine where we are on our pathways and we continuously monitor our movement toward cultural humility. It also describes concrete action steps that we can take to realize our desired outcomes as defined by our pathways. Collective book studies, engaging in culturally fortifying practices, and affinity group dialogues are all examples of equity pavers.

We cannot continue to blame kids and their families. We cannot ignore the hard truths that form our current realities. And, we cannot ignore or attempt to whitewash the historical systems of oppression that have plagued our communities. When we are confronted with the evidence

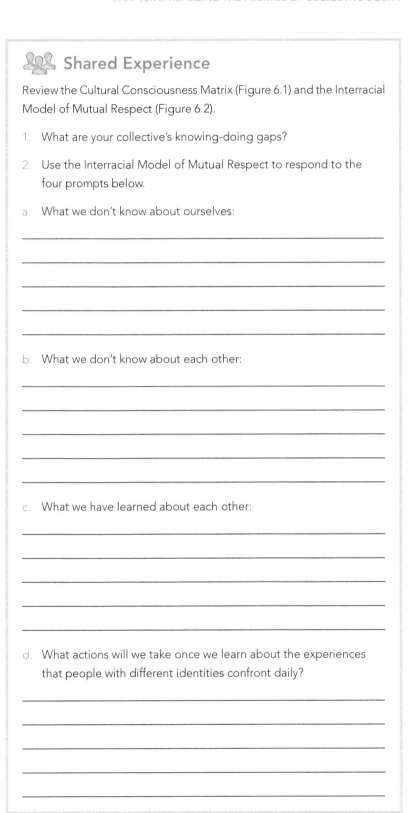

Shared Experience

Review the Cultural Consciousness Matrix (Figure 6.1) and the Interracial Model of Mutual Respect (Figure 6.2).

1. What are your collective's knowing-doing gaps?

2. Use the Interracial Model of Mutual Respect to respond to the four prompts below.

a. What we don't know about ourselves:

_____

_____

_____

_____

_____

b. What we don't know about each other:

_____

_____

_____

_____

_____

c. What we have learned about each other:

_____

_____

_____

_____

_____

d. What actions will we take once we learn about the experiences that people with different identities confront daily?

_____

_____

_____

_____

_____

of educational gaps, we must learn to acknowledge that such gaps are symptoms of a much greater problem. To transform the system, engagement in collective equity is everybody's business.

 Shared Experience

Reflecting on the responses to the prompts in the previous Shared Experience using the Interracial Model of Mutual Respect, what equity pavers (actions you will take) support the collective's ability to meet the following outcomes?

Celebrate and honor dimensions of identity:

_____

_____

_____

_____

_____

Understand each other and foster an appreciation of lived experiences:

_____

_____

_____

_____

_____

online resources   Available for download from resources.corwin.com/CollectiveEquity

Jot Thought

Now What? So What?

What does engagement of the collective look like to you?

_____

_____

_____

_____

online resources   Available for download from resources.corwin.com/CollectiveEquity

Summary

Transforming systems into collective equity demands courageous leadership and being conscious of where we are, our desired destination and the design of how we are going to get there. The leader of the collective masters the characteristics of relational leadership to design transformative equitable learning environments displaying the following attributes: authenticity, inclusivity, humility, and relatability. Leaders are important and have to have courage and immediacy with the members of the learning community to fortify them to make decisions and take actions to mitigate systems of oppression. When leaders come together and cultivate a shared focus with members of The Collective, they draw from the foundations of Collective Equity; The foundations of Collective Equity provide the structure to create equitable learning environments by leading, learning and convening in ways that are inclusive of all members of The Collective. We transform communities into equitable learning environments through participatory levels of knowing how to interact and engage with one another. Our journey starts with identifying equity pathways, and as we move toward equitable transformations, we leverage equity pavers to scaffold our movement.

Chapter Highlights

- Transforming the system demands leadership and being conscious of where we are, our desired destination, and the design of how we are going to get there.

- Collective equity calls on all members of the learning community to be active in transforming the system.

- Recognizing and confronting educational disparities that exist and persist in our schools demands honesty, strength, perseverance, and resilience to stay the course. It is so much easier to give up, but can we?

- The leader of the collective masters the characteristics of relational leadership. This requires a display of the following attributes: authenticity, inclusivity, humility, and relatability.

- When leaders come together and cultivate a shared focus with members of the collective, they draw from the foundations of collective equity.

- We must trouble existing systems, structures, policies, and practices of oppression and inequities by leading, learning, and convening in ways that are inclusive of all members of the collective.

- An equity pathway is a process of acquiring the knowledge, attitudes, and skills that act as a road map as we move toward equitable transformations.

- Our acknowledgment of where we are in each quadrant of the Cultural Consciousness Matrix signifies a starting place but does not determine where we end.

- An equity paver is a scaffold whereby we identify the prior knowledge, attitudes, and skills of the learning community; we determine where we are on the pathways and we continuously monitor our movement toward cultural humility.

Invitation to Collective Thinking

- As a leader, what are some goals and outcomes you have identified to create transformative equitable learning environments? How will you engage the members of the collective in acting upon these goals?

- How do you see the attributes of a collective equity leader being important to creating culturally fortifying learning environments?

- What are some of the inequities the members of the collective are committed to disrupting? What pathway will you identify to develop the knowledge and skills to disrupt these inequities?

Reflection

The Cultural Consciousness Matrix below outlines the levels of knowing that empower a collective to bridge the knowing-doing gap.

THE CULTURAL CONSCIOUSNESS MATRIX	
Level 2	Level 3
Consciously Unskilled	Consciously Skilled
• You know that you don't know	• You know that you have the skill
• Beginning of growth	• Comfortable with being uncomfortable
• Crisis of consciousness	• Focused confidence
• Enlightened	• Intentional
Being	**Becoming**
Level 1	Level 4
Unconsciously Unskilled	Unconsciously Skilled
• You don't know what you don't know	• You know the skill and the skill is second nature
• Complete lack of knowledge and skills	• Completely confident
• Fixed mindset	• Automaticity, accountability, humility
• Oblivious	• Graceful
Existing	**Evolving**

Source: Adapted from Burch (1970).

In what ways has the information in Chapter 6 closed your knowing-doing gap?

_____

_____

_____

_____

What is your knowing-doing gap?

_____

_____

_____

_____

So what does this mean for you?

_____

_____

_____

_____

Now what are your immediate actions?

_____

_____

_____

_____

Final Words
From the Authors

Simon Sinek (2012) tells you to start with your Why. This is our Why: At our very core, we are compelled to challenge the existing pervasive inequities that have plagued our communities.

Our conviction has bonded us to those who look like us, the clients who look to us, the children that we have served, the families that have depended on us, community members who put demands on us, teachers who partner with us, and principals who are empowered by us. We want to create spaces where all of these stakeholders have opportunities to unapologetically show up in the fullness of who they are.

Our inspiration comes from within and is fueled by our sense of urgency to disrupt the patterns of oppression and systems of inequity that intersect across race, diversity, class, and opportunity. Our own lived experiences of marginalization and exclusion, while painful, also keep us grounded, focused, and engaged in equity work. We have noticed that at times it does not matter who we are in our professional identities because when we show up as Black women, we often can't escape the distorted narratives that are vestiges of our American caste system (Wilkerson, 2020). These historical barriers and biases continue to feed unhealthy school climates, organizational conflict, lowered expectations, individual defensiveness, unwillingness to engage in self-examination, and fear of disturbing the status quo.

> *Whatever affects one directly, affects all indirectly. I can never be what I ought to be until you are what you ought to be. This is the interrelated structure of reality. (Dr. Martin Luther King, Jr.)*

We believe that the often-recited promise in the Pledge of Allegiance, "with liberty and justice for all," will never be realized if we don't come together.

We cannot do this work alone.

Our communities are depending on us to come together with humility, to put our individual interests aside, and to commit to fulfilling the promise of the Pledge. Collective equity is our response to dehumanization; the deleterious effects of culturally unresponsive environments; and continual degradation of Black, indigenous, and people of color (BIPOC), including students who don't feel safe enough to fully show up as who they are. As we fulfill the promises of collective equity, we strive to be proactive. Our learning communities have historically been reactive toward the inequities that continue to derail the fortifying experiences that all deserve. It is beyond time for us to acknowledge history and create spaces to mitigate the systemic "isms" that impact our schools every day.

If not us, then who? If not now, then when? (John Lewis)

Glossary

Collective Equity: a shared responsibility for the social, cultural, academic, and emotional fortification of students and adults that allows everyone to achieve their goals and aspirations on their own terms. It addresses systemic barriers, historic racism, educational disparities, and levels of oppression by fostering culturally fortifying experiences.

Collective Equity Dispositions: a required component of cultivating equitable learning environments. Our collective equity dispositions influence our decisions and the manner in which we choose (consciously or unconsciously) to interrogate or not interrogate systems of inequity.

Collective Equity Leader: a leader who demonstrates a genuineness and vulnerability to the connections they make within the learning community. Collective equity leaders recognize that equity transformation requires an endless learning journey embodying authenticity, relational trust, and a relentless focus on the acceleration of skills, knowledge, attitudes, and dispositions that inspire the collective to create equitable learning environments.

Community Agreements: a set of protocols or ground rules for guiding conversations and engagement in order to work in an environment with trust, purity, and authentic sincerity.

Constrained Equity: when growth stops and we are no longer conscious of our blind spots, which feeds the mindset of being culturally competent and "woke" and the belief that there is no need to grow and evolve.

Crisis of Consciousness: when people worry that they are not adept at having conversations around equity and engaging in equity work. It feeds into a process of self-blame and worry about intentions and character.

Culture: the beliefs, learned values, and behaviors that are shared by a community of people and ultimately make meaning of what happens with us and to us every day.

Cultural Humility: a lifelong process of learning to develop and enhance cultural knowledge requiring us to examine our cultural mental models and biases that inhibit us from experiencing all aspects of others.

Culturally Conscious: to understand that culture shapes us and that the privileges that we have been afforded and/or the oppression that we have experienced impact how we interact and engage with one another and the world around us.

Culturally Fortifying Practices: practices that recognize the strengths, assets, and the uniqueness that members of the learning community bring to the organization. When the members of the collective are fortified for who they are, they see, they hear, and they feel themselves in every aspect of the school culture.

Dot Inventory: a process used to ensure that every student is known in the learning community. Students names are posted around the room and teachers place dots on names of students where they have a significant relationship. This provides a visualization to making sure every student is known.

Enabling Conditions: an environment that empowers the collective to engage and affect the ways we work together to eliminate educational inequities.

Equity in Voice: the act of cultivating opportunities and spaces for all members of the learning community to communicate their thoughts and ideas while also being heard.

Equity Move: a plan of action to mitigate inequities, disparities, stereotypes, biased mindsets, oppressive policies, and exclusionary systems by incorporating high-yield evidence-based practices that culturally fortify members of the learning community.

Mirror Opportunities: materials, interactions, and opportunities in which students can see themselves and their cultures represented.

Shared Truths: the behaviors, beliefs, values, and realities that are agreed upon across an organization. Creating shared truths requires us to develop a common language, foster a community of trust, demonstrate authenticity, and honor equity in voice.

Unconstrained Equity: when one has an openness and capacity to appreciate differences; recognizes and owns the internal dissonance that comes along with challenges to what we have always known, believed, and valued; and has a personal and ongoing commitment to be better.

Window Opportunities: materials, interactions, and opportunities in which students can see authentic representations of different people and their diverse cultures.

References

Adger, N. (2003). Social capital, collective action, and adaptation to climate change. *Economic Geography, 79*(4), 387–404.

ASCD. (2019). Separate and still unequal: Race in America's schools [Special issue]. *Educational Leadership, 76*(7), 12–18.

Baker, M., Valentino-DeVries, J., Fernandez, M., & LaForgia, M. (2020, June 29). Three words. 70 cases. The tragic history of "I can't breathe." *The New York Times*. Retrieved June 30, 2020 from http://www.nytimes .com

Bandura, A. (1977). *Social learning theory.* Princeton, NJ: Princeton University Press.

Bandura, A. (1982). Self-efficacy mechanism in human agency. *American Psychologist, 37*(2), 122–147.

Bireda, M. (2011). Funding education equitably the "comparability provision" and the move to fair and transparent school budgeting systems. www.Americanpress.org.

Blackmore, J. (2009). International response essay leadership for social justice: A transnational dialogue. *Journal of Research on Leadership Education, 4*(1), 1–10.

Bloomberg, P., & Pitchford, B. (2016). *Leading impact teams: Building a culture of efficacy.* Thousand Oaks, CA: Corwin.

Bolton, G., & Delderfield, R. (2018). *Reflective practice: Writing and professional development.* Thousand Oaks, CA: SAGE.

Brown, B. (2012). *Daring greatly: how the courage to be vulnerable transforms the way we live, love, parent, and lead.* New York: Random house.

Bryk, A., & Schneider, B. (2002). *Trust in schools: A core resource for improvement.* New York: Russell Sage Foundation.

Bryk, A., & Schneider, B. (2003). Trust in schools: A core resource for school reform. *Educational Leadership, 60*(6), 40–45.

Carroll, D. (2007). Developing dispositions for ambitious teaching. *Journal of Educational Controversy, 2*(2). Article 7.

Chotiner, I. (2020). Bryan Stevenson on the frustration behind the George Floyd protests. *The New Yorker*. Retrieved from https://www.newyorker.com/news/q-and-a/bryan-stevenson-on-the-frustration-behind-the-george-floyd-protests

Chugh, D. (2018). *The person you mean to be: How good people fight bias.* Harper Collins.

Comer, D., & Sekerka, L. (2014). Keep calm and carry on (ethically): Durable moral courage in the workplace. *Human Resource Management Review, 28*(2), 116–130.

Covey, S. (2006). *The speed of trust: The one thing that changes everything.* New York: Free Press.

Crenshaw, K. (1989). Demarginalizing the intersection of race and sex: A black feminist critique of antidiscrimination doctrine, feminist theory and antiracist politics. *University of Chicago Legal Forum, 1989,* 1.

Darling-Hammond, L. (2018). *Kerner at 50: Educational equity still a dream deferred.* Retrieved from http://learningpolicyinstitute.org

Davis, B., & Anderson, K. (2010). *Creating culturally considerate schools: Educating without bias.* Thousand Oaks, CA: Corwin.

de Brey, C., Musu, L., McFarland, J., Wilkinson-Flicker, S., Diliberti, M., Zhang, A., Branstetter, C., & Wang, X. (2019). *Status* and trends in the education of racial and ethnic groups 2018 (NCES 2019–038). Washington, DC: National Center for Education Statistics. Retrieved from https://nces.ed.gov

Eacott, S. (2018). *Beyond leadership.* New York: Springer.

Education Week Research Center (2019). *Analysis of NCES data.*

Equity and Excellence Commission. (2018). *For each and every child.* ED Pubs Education Publications Center, U.S. Department of Education.

Fisher, D., Frey, N., Almarode, J., Flories, K., & Nagel, D. (2019). *PLC+ Better decisions and greater impact by design.* Thousand Oaks, CA: Corwin.

Fisher, D., Frey, N., & Hattie, J. (2016). *Visible learning for literacy, grades K–12: Implementing the practices that work best to accelerate student learning.* Thousand Oaks, CA: Corwin.

Fisher, D., Frey, N., & Smith, D. (2020). *The distance learning playbook for school leaders: Leading for engagement and impact in any setting.* Thousand Oaks, CA: Corwin.

Fullan, M. (2009). *The challenge of change: Start school improvement now!* Thousand Oaks, CA: Corwin.

Fullan, M. (2012). *Motion leadership in action: More skinny on becoming change savvy.* Thousand Oaks, CA: Corwin.

Fullan, M. (2021). *The right drivers for whole system success* (CSE Leading Education Series, 01). Melbourne, AU: Centre for Strategic Education.

Fullan, M., & Gallagher, M. J. (2020). *The devil is in the details: System solutions for equity, excellence, and student well-being.* Thousand Oaks, CA: Corwin.

Fullan, M., & Quinn, J. (2016). *The taking action guide to building coherence in schools, districts, and systems.* Thousand Oaks, CA: Corwin.

Gamoran, A. (2001). American schooling and educational inequality: A forecast for the 21st century. *Sociology of Education, 74,* 135–153.

Gay, G. (2010). *Culturally responsive teaching: Theory, research, and practice.* New York: Teachers College Press.

Gleason, T. (2020). *Trust is contagious: The role of trust in school relationships and teacher retention rates* (138) [Doctoral dissertation, St. John's University]. https://scholar.stjohns.edu/theses_dissertations/138

Goffee, R., & Jones, G. (2005). Managing authenticity: The paradox of great leadership. *Harvard Business Review, 83*(12), 86–94.

Gorski, P. (2019). *Taco night.* Retrieved from http://www.EquityLiteracy.org

Gorski, P., & Pothini, S. (2018). *Case studies on diversity and social justice education.* London: Routledge.

Gruenert, S., & Whittaker, T. (2015). *School culture rewired: How to define, assess, and transform it.* Alexandria, VA: ASCD.

Hall, D., & Ushomirsky, N. (2010). Close the hidden funding gaps in our schools. *Education Trust.*

Hammond, Z. (2015). *Culturally responsive teaching and the brain: Promoting authentic engagement and rigor among culturally and linguistically diverse students.* Thousand Oaks, CA: Corwin.

Hargreaves, A., & Fullan, M. (2012). *The global fourth way: The quest for educational excellence.* Thousand Oaks, CA: Corwin.

Harris, A. (2010). Leading system transformation. *School Leadership & Management, 30*(4), 197–207.

Hattie, J., & Zierer, K. (2017). *10 mindframes for visible learning: Teaching for success.* London: Routledge.

Hattie, J. (2012). *Visible learning for teachers* New York: Routledge.

Heifetz, R., Grashow, A., & Linsky, M. (2009). *The practice of adaptive leadership: Tools and tactics for changing your organization and the world.* Boston, MA: Harvard Business.

History of PLC. (2021). *All things PLC.* Retrieved July 12, 2021 from https://www.allthingsplc.info/about/history-of-plc

Hofstede, G. (1980). *Culture's consequences: International differences in work-related values.* Thousand Oaks, CA: SAGE.

Howard, G. (2015). *We can't lead where we won't go: An educator's guide to equity.* Thousand Oaks, CA: Corwin.

Howard, L. (2016). *Bright ribbons: Weaving culturally responsive teaching into the elementary classroom* Thousand Oaks, CA: Corwin.

Hoy, W., & Tschannen-Moran, M. (1999). Five faces of trust: An empirical confirmation in urban elementary schools. *Journal of School Leadership, 9,* 184–208.

Jackson, Y. (2015). Rewriting the script in urban schools. *Educational Leadership, 72,* 14–21.

Ladson-Billings, G. (1995). Toward a theory of culturally relevant pedagogy. *American Educational Research Journal, 32*(3), 465–491.

Le, V. (2017). Equity fatigue and how it affects leaders of color. *Changemakers Blog.* Retrieved from https://rvcseattle.org/2017/08/02/equity-fatigue-affects-leaders-color/

Marzano, R. (2003). *What works in schools: Translating research into action.* Alexandria, VA: ASCD.

Maslow, A. (1943). A Theory of Human Motivation - Psychological Review Vol 50, no 4

Maxwell, J. (2019, May 21). Want better relationships? Be relatable! [Blog post]. Retrieved from https://www.johnmaxwell.com/blog/want-better-relationships-be-relatable/

McFarland, J., Hussar, B., Zhang, J., Wang, X., Wang, K., Hein, S., Diliberti, M., Forrest Cataldi, E., Bullock Mann, F., and Barmer, A. (2019). The Condition of Education, Educational Week Research Center - National Center for Education Statistices. Retrieved September 8, 2021 from The Condition of Education 2019

Myers, V. (2016). *Diversity without inclusion misses the point.* Retrieved July 12, 2021 from https://www.vernamyers.com/2016/06/09/diversity-without-inclusion-misses-the-point/

National Council for Accreditation of Teacher Education. (2002). *Professional standards for the accreditation of schools, colleges, and departments of education.* Washington, DC: Author.

National School Boards Association. (2020). Retrieved July 13, 2021 from https://nsba.org/

Newman, G.E. & Smith, R. K (2016). Kinds of Authenticity. https://doi.org/10.1111/phc3.12343

Orfield, G., & Eaton, S. (1996). *Dismantling desegregation: The quiet reversal of Brown v. Board of Education.* New York: The New Press.

Paez, M. & Albert, L. R. (2012). Cultural consciousness. In J. A. Banks (Ed), *Encyclopedia of diversity in education.* Thousand Oaks, CA: SAGE Publications

Palmer, P. (2004). *A hidden wholeness: The journey toward an undivided life.* San Francisco, CA: Jossey-Bass.

Palmer, P. (2012). *The courage to teach: Exploring the inner landscape of a teacher's life.* San Francisco, CA: Jossey-Bass.

Pink, D. (2009). *Drive: The surprising truth about what motivates us.* New York: Riverhead Books.

Pretty, J., & Ward, H. (2001). Social capital and the environment. *World Development, 29*(2), 209–227.

Purkey, W., & Novak, J. (2015). *An introduction to invitational theory.* Retrieved from https://www.invitationaleducation.org/resources/

Race Matters Institute. (2014). *Racial equity transforms organizations.* Retrieved from https://viablefuturescenter.org/racemattersinstitute/

Radke, H., Kutlaca, M., Siem, B., Wright, S., & Becker, J. (2020). Beyond allyship: Motivations for advantaged group members to engage in action for disadvantaged groups. *Journal of Personality and Social Review, 24*(4), 291–315.

Reeves, D. (2006). *The learning leader: How to focus on school improvement for better results.* Alexandria, VA: ASCD.

Robbins, S. P. (2005). *Essentials of organizational behavior* (8th ed.). Upper Saddle River, NJ: Prentice Hall.

Safir, S., & Dugan, J. (2021). *Street data: A next-generation model for equity, pedagogy, and school transformation.* Thousand Oaks, CA: Corwin.

Scheurich, J., & Skrla, L. (2003). *Creating high-achievement classrooms, schools and districts.* Thousand Oaks, CA: Corwin.

Shade, B., Kelly, C., & Oberg, M. (1997). *Creating culturally responsive classrooms.* Washington, DC: American Psychological Association.

Simmons, D. (2019). How to be an antiracist educator. *ASDC Education Update, 61*(10).

Sinek, S. (2012). *Start with why: How great leaders inspire everyone to take action.* London, UK: Penguin.

Sugarman, M. Sullard, J. & Wilhem,, E. (2011). *The 8 dimensions of leadership: DISC strategies for becoming a better leader.* San Francisco, CA: Berrett-Koehler Publishers.

Tatum, G. (2017). *Why are all the black kids sitting together in the cafeteria? And other conversations about race.* New York: Basic Books.

Taylor Tricomi, E. (1986). Krashen's second-language acquisition theory and the teaching of edited American English. *Journal of Basic Writing, 5*(2), 59–69.

Tervalon, M., & Murray-Garcia, J. (1998). Cultural humility vs cultural competence: A critical distinction in defining physician training outcomes in multicultural education. *Journal of Health Care for the Poor and Underserved, 9*(2), 117–125.

Thornton, H. (2006). Dispositions in action: Do dispositions make a difference in practice? *Teacher Education Quarterly, 33*(2), 53–68.

Tschannen-Moran, M. (2003). Fostering organizational citizenship: Transformational leadership and trust. In W. K. Hoy & C. G. Miskel (Eds.), *Studies in leading and organizing schools* (pp. 157–179). Greenwich, CT: Information Age.

Tschannen-Moran, M., & Gareis, C. (2015). Faculty trust in the principal: An essential ingredient in high-performing schools. *Journal of Educational Administration, 53*(1), 66–92.

von Frank, V. (2010). A learning community is built on trust. *The Learning Principal, 4*(7), 1, 6–7.

Wilkerson, I. (2020). *Caste: The origins of our discontents.* New York: Random House.

Index

A SAGE Publishing Company

Helping educators make the greatest impact

CORWIN HAS ONE MISSION: to enhance education through intentional professional learning.

We build long-term relationships with our authors, educators, clients, and associations who partner with us to develop and continuously improve the best evidence-based practices that establish and support lifelong learning.